THE
GENERAL
EPISTLES

An Exposition

by
CHARLES R. ERDMAN

PREFACE BY EARL F. ZEIGLER

THE WESTMINSTER PRESS

PHILADELPHIA

Published by The Westminster Press®
Philadelphia, Pennsylvania

PRINTED IN THE UNITED STATES OF AMERICA

To
My Mother

CONTENTS

CONTENTS

PREFACE

Seven letters in the New Testament have long been grouped together and named "The General (or Catholic) Epistles." They are in the order in which they appear: James, I Peter, II Peter, I John, II John, III John, and Jude. In combined wordage they are about the length of I Corinthians. The longest is I Peter, the shortest are II John and III John which are almost equal. A rapid reader can complete the entire seven letters in less than an hour, whether the reading is silent or aloud. Anyone who has never read this group of seven at a sitting may find the experience quite revealing.

Exactly why Biblical scholars have named this group "General" or "Catholic" is conjecture. Their content is, broadly speaking, of a "general" nature. The people to whom the letters are addressed may also be thought of as "general." But neither of these reasons holds completely. The name was given perhaps centuries ago; the name has stuck. It is not likely to be changed.

For purpose of publication in this Erdman series of New Testament commentaries, it was decided to include in one volume all seven of the letters, and issue the volume under the title, THE GENERAL EPISTLES. A glance at the Contents will indicate the arrangement of the material for the student's use. There is an Introduction to the entire seven letters, followed by an introductory statement on The Epistle of James. The text of James is then interpreted by the expositor, Dr. Charles R. Erdman, according to the outline he adopted. The same pattern is then followed for the remaining six letters.

Those who have consulted any of the other volumes in this series of commentaries, seventeen in all, know that Dr. Charles R. Erdman has authored all of them. He completed the series while he was professor of practical theology in Princeton Seminary. (A portion of this period he was also pastor of the First Presbyterian Church in Princeton; and previously he had held two pastorates in Philadelphia.) His exposition of the New Testament books has been so popular that continued printings were necessary. Type and plates finally yielded to wear, and a completely new set were created for this present paperback edition.

Dr. Erdman takes the position that four different authors wrote the seven letters. James and Jude, brothers of Jesus, wrote the two bearing their names. Peter and John, disciples of Jesus, wrote the five bearing their names. Many Biblical scholars would agree *in toto* with the Erdman working conclusion; while other scholars of repute have questioned this view. In such matters as authorship, many students do not like to have traditional positons disturbed, but others find satisfaction in consulting the scholars who are constantly conducting research to discover, if possible, more factual material from which to draw conclusions about authorship and other salient concerns. No matter what "authorities" are consulted, the student will find other "authorities" who produce evidence that must be considered.

Dr. Erdman, it will be learned by the reader of this volume, takes a minimum of space to state his position on unresolved questions. He takes the positive approach that delves into the text of the New Testament writing that he may bring forth its timely and timeless teaching. In the exposition of these seven letters Dr. Erdman has placed before the student what he believes the letters were intended to teach those to whom they were addressed, and what they teach to us who read and study them now.

EARL F. ZEIGLER

FOREWORD

Here are strengthening words for days of storm and testing, and cheering words for nights dark and starless, and guiding words for times of mental perplexity and of moral peril. They come to us across distant centuries, but they meet precisely our modern needs. They are weighted with divine mysteries, but they chiefly concern human duties. They were addressed to members of a heavenly brotherhood, but they deal with the practical, earthly problems of employers and servants, husbands and wives, teachers and taught, rich and poor, of all who need encouragement to press on through sorrow to joy, through temptation and failure to strength and victory, through doubts and fears to assured faith and cloudless hope. They were written by men who had been companions of Christ, but they are his present messengers for all who yield to his Spirit and seek to do his will.

INTRODUCTION

The art of letter writing has been lost; at least it is seldom displayed. The haste of modern life, the many means of communication, the ease of travel and transportation, the multitude of books and papers, these and other causes have increased vastly the volume of correspondence, but have made its character more fugitive and less studied and serious. It cannot be denied, however, that this form of literature is peculiarly instinct with human interest and rich in biographic and historical material.

Among all the letters of the world, those written in the first century by the followers of Christ, and preserved for us in the New Testament, are regarded as supreme. By way of eminence they are called epistles. This word, of course, might be applied to any series of letters; yet fortunately its use is being restricted to these which have exercised such an incomparable influence upon men.

Of these epistles those which bear the names of James, Peter, John, and Jude have been placed in a group by themselves and for many centuries have been known as the catholic or "General Epistles." The exact meaning of the title has been a matter of some uncertainty. It may refer to their authorship, their contents, or their destination. The authorship of all other New Testament epistles has popularly been assigned to Paul, but in this group of General Epistles we find the products of a number of different writers. Of these, James and Jude were own brothers of Jesus and the other two, Peter and John, were his most prominent apostles. It is of interest to note that we find here the writings of two men who had shared the experiences of the home in Nazareth and of two other men, who had been most intimate with Christ in the days of his earthly ministry and who after his ascension were most closely united in the work of establishing his church.

While it is not highly probable that the title of these epistles is due to their content, it is true that the themes discussed are of the most general character. They contain references to every cardinal doctrine of Christianity, and touch every phase of Christian experience. It is well to note, however, that each one of these writers lays special stress upon some one characteristic and distinguishing truth. James is the apostle of works, Peter gives messages of hope, John is an exponent of love, and Jude emphasizes the need of a pure faith.

It is most of all likely that the title is due to the general character of the readers for whom these epistles were designed. Paul wrote his letters to specific individuals or churches or groups of churches; these letters were addressed to the universal church or to Christian believers scattered over wide areas of the Roman Empire. This is not strictly true of them all. For example, the Second and Third Epistles of John seem to be addressed to individuals. However, it is sufficiently accurate to suggest this general character as the origin of the familiar title and to make us feel that here are messages designed for the guidance of Christians in every place and time.

The historic references in these epistles lead us back to the earthly ministry of Christ and to the recorded acts of his apostles. The prophetic utterances point us forward to his return, not with such fullness as to satisfy our curiosity, but with such certainty as to inspire hope. One of their chief values lies in their accurate pictures of the apostolic church, covering the whole course of its career from the early ministry of James to the late years of the aged John. The passages of difficult interpretation are sufficiently numerous to inspire humility and caution; but the main teachings are plain and of immediate application to the life and problems of the modern church. They invite careful and repeated reading and suggest the possibility of continual growth "in the grace and knowledge of our Lord and Saviour Jesus Christ."

THE EPISTLE OF JAMES

THE EPISTLE OF JAMES

Those were peculiar privileges which the writer of this epistle enjoyed during the long years of companionship with Jesus, his brother, in the home of Mary at Nazareth; together they read the book of nature in lovely Galilee, together they were taught the Book of God by their mother and in the village school. These influences were never lost. It is true that, like his brothers, James did not understand the startling claims which Jesus made as he began his public ministry, he was not convinced by the miracles or the equally wonderful messages of our Lord; he illustrates the stupidity, possibly the subsequent poignant regret, of those who fail to value the familiar and the near, and who give no honor to a prophet "in his own house." Nevertheless he never lost the impression made upon him by the words and works of Christ; and when, in the light of the resurrection, the light which alone brings conviction to most of us today, he saw the true nature of his brother according to the flesh, he was ready to worship and serve him as his divine Lord and Master. Then those early influences bore their abundant fruit. No one among the followers of Christ was better known, none more respected, none more honored. James was conceded the place of leadership, he was recognized as the head of the church. So, too, as he composed his epistle he used, more nearly than any other writer, the very words of Jesus, and he reproduced more perfectly the spirit of those Scriptures which as a boy he had studied with Jesus.

It is evident from the letter that those whom James addresses were Jews. He calls them "the twelve tribes which are of the Dispersion," and he has in mind his fellow countrymen who were scattered in various parts of the Roman world. Evidently they have accepted Jesus as the

Messiah, as "the Lord of glory," and James is writing from Jerusalem to urge them to live in accordance with their Christian profession. Most of them seem to be poor, and to be suffering from the selfishness and oppression of the Jews among whom they are living. They are persecuted as apostates, dragged before the judgment seats, imprisoned, deprived of their goods, and tempted to renounce their faith. Nor are they themselves free from fault. They seek the friendship of the world, are obsequious to the rich, are at strife among themselves, are lacking in Christian love. The purpose of the epistle, therefore, is eminently practical. James seeks to correct their errors and to admonish them for their failures. He does not attempt to teach Christian doctrine, but to stimulate Christian life. He assumes the great truths of the faith and upon these as a foundation urges the readers to build the necessary superstructure of consistent works.

The theme of the epistle might be stated as "Christian Wisdom," by which is meant, not speculative knowledge or revealed truth, but practical knowledge, truth applied to life, creed resulting in character. It shows how Christians should and may live in days of discouragement and persecution; it suggests the temptations by which they ever are beset. It guides their actions when trials abound, when even in churches may be found "respect of persons," dead orthodoxy, tongues of deceit, evil speaking, love of the world, forgetfulness of God, self-indulgence, and greed. It is thus an epistle of practical wisdom for perilous times.

Most striking of all is the fact that its fundamental note voices the universal cry of the present age. This note is the demand for reality in religion; it rebukes all pretense and self-deception, all sham and hypocrisy; it insists that faith shall be tested by works, that character shall correspond to profession. It is this underlying thought which unites the various sections of the epistle and brings into vital relation its diverse themes. These sections may be summarized as follows:

THE GENERAL EPISTLES

An Exposition

I
TRIALS AND TEMPTATIONS

JAMES 1:1-18

*1 James, a servant of God and of the Lord Jesus Christ,
to the twelve tribes which are of the Dispersion, greeting.*

*2 Count it all joy, my brethren, when ye fall into mani-
fold temptations; 3 knowing that the proving of your faith
worketh patience. 4 And let patience have* its *perfect work,
that ye may be perfect and entire, lacking in nothing.*

*5 But if any of you lacketh wisdom, let him ask of God,
who giveth to all liberally and upbraideth not; and it shall
be given him. 6 But let him ask in faith, nothing doubting:
for he that doubteth is like the surge of the sea driven by
the wind and tossed. 7 For let not that man think that
he shall receive anything of the Lord; 8 a doubleminded
man, unstable in all his ways.*

*9 But let the brother of low degree glory in his high
estate: 10 and the rich, in that he is made low: because as
the flower of the grass he shall pass away. 11 For the sun
ariseth with the scorching wind, and withereth the grass;
and the flower thereof falleth, and the grace of the fashion
of it perisheth: so also shall the rich man fade away in
his goings.*

*12 Blessed is the man that endureth temptation; for
when he hath been approved, he shall receive the crown
of life, which* the Lord *promised to them that love him.
13 Let no man say when he is tempted, I am tempted of
God; for God cannot be tempted with evil, and he himself
tempteth no man: 14 but each man is tempted, when he is
drawn away by his own lust, and enticed. 15 Then the
lust, when it hath conceived, beareth sin: and the sin, when
it is fullgrown, bringeth forth death. 16 Be not deceived,
my beloved brethren. 17 Every good gift and every perfect gift is from above, coming down from the Father of
lights, with whom can be no variation, neither shadow that*

is cast by turning. 18 Of his own will he brought us forth by the word of truth, that we should be a kind of firstfruits of his creatures.

In his brief line of greeting James pauses for no long description of himself or of his readers, merely indicating that as a "servant of God" he worships and obeys Jesus Christ as divine Lord and Master, and that those to whom he writes are Jews of the great national Dispersion. He at once turns to the first great need of the readers, both in his day and ours, as he gives comfort in trial and warning in temptation. It is true that both experiences are denoted by the same word, yet the testing of which he speaks first is that of outward circumstances, and that which he next considers is due to inward desire.

He startles us by the strange paradox with which he begins, as he bids us "count it all joy" when we are suddenly overwhelmed by misfortunes of every possible kind. He does not mean that we are to court disaster or to seek for trouble or to deny the reality of pain and sorrow, but we are to regard all these adversities as tests of faith and as means of moral and spiritual growth. We are to rejoice, not because distresses come, but in view of their possible results. They may produce "patience," which is not mere passive submission, but steadfast endurance and triumphant trust. We are urged therefore to allow "patience" to do its full work in producing a maturity of character in which every virtue is fully developed and no grace is lacking. Such a blessed issue of trials is possible only when we look upon them in the right light; it requires "wisdom" to see life steadily and "see it whole" and to view its darker scenes in their right perspective. Trials may embitter, they may dwarf, they may work moral disaster. Therefore we must ask God for needed grace, for true "wisdom." He gives to all liberally; he never rebukes us for asking too much. We must, however, look to him in absolute confidence. If our minds are allowed to dwell only on our

distress, or to turn restlessly back and forth from his
changeless love to our pitiful selves, the state of the soul
is like a wave of the sea, "driven by the wind and tossed";
surely, then, no divine grace can be received, no moral
progress can be made.

Two familiar examples of testing are now given: the
trials of poverty and the temptations of wealth. Either
may result in moral injury, even in spiritual disaster; but
if met with the "wisdom" which God gives, either may
issue in the perfecting of character. It is of course much
easier to rejoice when wealth comes than when it goes;
but joy may be possible in the latter experience when we
realize that what one is should concern him more than
what he has, particularly when we remember that wealth
passes away and a man ceases to be rich quite as swiftly as
a flower withers under the summer sun. The character,
however, which issues, from either the test of prosperity
or the test of adversity, abides forever.

As James, therefore, emphasizes the reward of endurance, he speaks of "the crown of life, which the Lord
promised to them that love him," by which he means that
one whose faith stands the test, one who views each event
of life in the light of the wisdom which God gives, receives
as a reward, as an inevitable result, life in ever fuller,
larger degree, life more abundant, life for time and for
eternity.

As the writer declares this blessedness of "the man that
endureth temptation," he has in mind both the tests of
outward circumstances and also of inclinations to sin. Of
the latter he now speaks in more detail. He assures us
that as trials may lead into truer life, any harm which results from them must be due to the evil within us. That
which converts a trial into a temptation is solely the sinful
lust that comes from our own hearts. "Let no man say
when he is tempted, I am tempted of God." We may not
use those words, but we are all inclined to excuse our
wrongdoing on the ground of some circumstance or in-

heritance which is logically related to the providence of God, which therefore comes from God. Evil, however, cannot tempt God, it can make no appeal to him, it cannot have its source in him; therefore "he himself tempteth no man." Evil desire, which we should resist, which by the grace of God we may resist, is like a temptress by whom one is coaxed and cajoled and enticed; and when evil desire is allowed to lodge in the heart it soon controls the will. The result is sin, and the issue of sin is nothing less hideous than death. The loss of beauty and purity and holiness and happiness, the loss of fellowship with goodness and God, the loss of all that is worthy the name of life, comes from our own evil selves.

James warns us against false conceptions of ourselves or of God: "Be not deceived, my beloved brethren." So far from being the author of evil, God is the Giver of every good gift, and all his gifts are good. He is like the sun; other heavenly bodies like the moon or stars may wax or wane, but from "the Father of lights" streams forth changeless, unmingled love. Surely we can trust him in every hour of trial, in every time of temptation. His greatest gift is the new life which he has imparted to us through the truth revealed in Christ. As the "firstfruits" were dedicated to God and gave promise of the coming harvest, so we Christians are designed to be the special possession of God and the pledge and earnest of a redeemed race.

II
HEARING AND DOING
Ch. 1:19-27

19 Ye know this, my beloved brethren. But let every man be swift to hear, slow to speak, slow to wrath: 20 for the wrath of man worketh not the righteousness of God. 21 Wherefore putting away all filthiness and overflowing of wickedness, receive with meekness the implanted word, which is able to save your souls. 22 But be ye doers of the word, and not hearers only, deluding your own selves. 23 For if any one is a hearer of the word and not a doer, he is like unto a man beholding his natural face in a mirror: 24 for he beholdeth himself, and goeth away, and straight- way forgetteth what manner of man he was. 25 But he that looketh into the perfect law, the law of liberty, and so continueth, being not a hearer that forgetteth but a doer that worketh, this man shall be blessed in his doing. 26 If any man thinketh himself to be religious, while he bridleth not his tongue but deceiveth his heart, this man's religion is vain. 27 Pure religion and undefiled before our God and Father is this, to visit the fatherless and widows in their affliction, and to keep oneself unspotted from the world.

James has been speaking of the word of God as the instrument whereby a new life is imparted to the believer. He intimates that his readers are familiar with this fact, and with the gracious purpose of God toward all men: "Ye know this, my beloved brethren." He deems it neces- sary, however, to give certain instructions relative to the use which should be made of this word of God, this "word of truth," this gospel message. In fact, he reaches the central thought of his epistle as he insists that truth must be received into the heart and expressed in the life. There are those who seem to think that "the word" is intended as an object about which we are to talk or to fight. Some men find little else in the Bible than subjects for debate. On the contrary, James insists that the message concerning Christ must be heard with eagerness and carefully obeyed. "Let every man be swift to hear," let him improve every opportunity for learning more truth, let him listen again and again to the divine message, let him be ready to receive light from any source. Let him be "slow to speak," humbly taking the place of a learner, or if it becomes his duty to testify or to teach, let him do so with modesty and reverence, avoiding all carelessness and flippancy and self-confidence. Let him also be "slow to wrath." Unhappily religious discussions are too often attended with heat and anger. Too many public teachers seem to feel that the bitterness with which they assail their opponents will attest their zeal and devotion. James reminds such that "the wrath of man" cannot produce "the righteousness" which God requires and which he aims to produce in the conduct of Christians. True hearers will put away all evil and malicious thoughts, and by a spirit of meekness will prepare the soul, as good soil, for the reception of "the word," which is implanted like good seed and springs up in a harvest of virtue and holiness and life.

That this blessed issue may result, the believer must receive the truth not only with meekness but also with prompt and resolute obedience: "But be ye doers of the word, and not hearers only, deluding your own selves." This delusion is common in the case of those who suppose themselves to be religious because they are familiar with religious truths and their discussion. One who merely listens, or whose knowledge results in no action, is likened by James to a man who gives a hasty glance into a mirror and then turns away forgetful of what he has seen and with no effort toward improving his appearance. What a magic mirror the Word of God provides! It shows a man exactly what he is, with all his faults and failures and infirmities; and yet, as he gazes upon that reflection, he beholds another image, that of the ideal Man, and he sees what he himself should be. Most marvelous of all, as he looks steadfastly upon the glorious perfection of his Lord, he finds himself free from the bondage of habit and self and sin, and becoming "transformed into the same image from glory to glory." Surely, one who makes such a use of the word of truth, one who gazes into it and makes its revelations the law of his life, cannot fail to find the blessing of God on all his deeds; he is "not a hearer that forgetteth but a doer that worketh."

James has suggested that a man may deceive himself as to his religious state by his enjoyment of religious discussions, or by his fluency of speech on religious themes, or by the warmth of his passion in religious disputes; he now adds that another cause of self-deception may be found in the care with which one performs religious rites and ceremonies. One may be most scrupulous in observing all the prescribed forms of religion, he may give alms and pray and fast, as the Pharisees did; he may attend church and sing hymns and observe sacraments; but his religion may still be an empty and vain delusion. James suggests three tests of religion, or to follow his words more exactly, he prescribes three religious exercises which cannot fail to please God.

The first of these is self-control. The example which he gives is that of ability to bridle the tongue. In contrast with those members of the church who prided themselves upon their skill in debate and their ability to distress their opponents, he suggests that a truer test of religion may be found in the ability to keep silence, particularly under irritating and annoying circumstances. "Holding the tongue" is only one of many forms of self-discipline, but, as James suggests in a later chapter, it is a supreme test, and, "if any stumbleth not in word, the same is a perfect man, able to bridle the whole body."

The second exercise of religion which James proposes is charity. As the Old Testament frequently intimates, those usually most in need of sympathy and aid are orphans and widows. But they are not the only persons who make their appeal to our pity; James mentions them simply as types or examples; but he declares that care for them constitutes a true religious ceremony, it is part of a real ritual: "Pure religion and undefiled before our God and Father is this, to visit the fatherless and widows in their affliction."

The third expression of religion mentioned by James is purity: "To keep oneself unspotted from the world." To be religious, in this true sense, is by no means easy. The world about us is full of evil; its maxims, its practices, its ideals, are too commonly opposed to the will of God. By obedience to them the pure soul is sullied and stained by sin. To walk "in white garments," to have clean hands and clean hearts, this is to be religious, this is to please God.

III
RESPECT OF PERSONS

Ch. 2:1-13

1 My brethren, hold not the faith of our Lord Jesus Christ, the Lord of glory, with respect of persons. 2 For if there come into your synagogue a man with a gold ring, in fine clothing, and there come in also a poor man in vile clothing; 3 and ye have regard to him that weareth the fine clothing, and say, Sit thou here in a good place; and ye say to the poor man, Stand thou there, or sit under my footstool; 4 do ye not make distinctions among yourselves, and become judges with evil thoughts? 5 Hearken, my beloved brethren; did not God choose them that are poor as to the world to be rich in faith, and heirs of the kingdom which he promised to them that love him? 6 But ye have dishonored the poor man. Do not the rich oppress you, and themselves drag you before the judgment-seats? 7 Do not they blaspheme the honorable name by which ye are called? 8 Howbeit if ye fulfil the royal law, according to the scripture, Thou shalt love thy neighbor as thyself, ye do well: 9 but if ye have respect of persons, ye commit sin, being convicted by the law as transgressors. 10 For whosoever shall keep the whole law, and yet stumble in one point, he is become guilty of all. 11 For he that said, Do not commit adultery, said also, Do not kill. Now if thou dost not commit adultery, but killest, thou art become a transgressor of the law. 12 So speak ye, and so do, as men that are to be judged by a law of liberty. 13 For judgment is without mercy to him that hath showed no mercy: mercy glorieth against judgment.

In his first chapter, James has spoken of the temptations by which we are assailed; here he deals with one which is most common, namely, that of partiality, of making unfair distinctions between persons. He has also referred to

"the word of truth" by which we should direct our lives;
he here mentions a fault which the law of Christ would
forbid. Possibly the connection is even more direct. The
previous verses have dealt with forms of religious service;
here the writer may be recalling a scene which he had re-
cently witnessed in the place of worship. The incident,
whether real or imaginary, was one in which honor was
shown to a rich man and disrespect to a man who was
poor; it is here mentioned to illustrate the fault which
James seeks to correct, namely, "respect of persons."
The word so translated means "judging by appearances,"
and so influenced to unfair treatment of people by considerations of wealth or class or power or social distinction.
The folly of such behavior is rebuked by the words the
writer employs to introduce his theme: "My brethren."
We should treat one another as equals in the household of
God and "hold not the faith of our Lord Jesus Christ, the
Lord of glory, with respect of persons." As our faith is in
Jesus Christ, we should follow his example; as we submit
to him as Lord, we should obey his law; as he is "the Lord
of glory," then, by comparison with him, all degrees of
rank and position among men are insignificant and con-
temptible.

Nevertheless, the fault of partiality, and of making unjust distinctions, is far too common even among Christians. Few of us find the least difficulty in imagining the
picture which James paints: Two strangers present themselves to take part in a religious service; one, by his
gorgeous clothing and his jewelry, is proclaimed to be rich;
the other, in wretched rags, is evidently poor; the former
is cordially welcomed and given a seat of honor, the latter
is made to stand against the wall or to crouch upon the
floor. Such conduct and all similar offenses James severely
rebukes: "Do ye not make distinctions among yourselves,
and become judges with evil thoughts?"

The fault is condemned as unreasonable. It is really
absurd. Many poor men are actually rich, and many

rich men are deserving only of contempt. How foolish
then to judge a man by outward circumstances or to condemn him because he belongs to a certain class! Poor
men are often peculiarly rich in faith, and heirs of the
glorious Kingdom of God; rich men are often opposed to
God and his cause. The latter, in the days of James, were
notoriously cruel to Christians, oppressing them and drag-
ging them to the judgment seats, and blaspheming the
name of their Lord.

More serious still the fault is not only unreasonable;
it is unlawful, it is actually sinful. For all Christians, and
in the treatment of all men there is one changeless law:
it is the law of love. It is called "the royal law" because
it is superior to all others and because it makes those who
obey it regal and kingly. It is called the "law of liberty"
for it sets men free from sin and self. If we are controlled
by this law in our treatment of rich or poor, we are worthy
of praise; "If ye fulfil the royal law, according to the scripture, Thou shalt love thy neighbor as thyself, ye do well:
but if ye have respect of persons, ye commit sin, being convicted by the law as transgressors."

To emphasize the guilt James adds the difficult words:
"For whosoever shall keep the whole law, and yet stumble
in one point, he is become guilty of all." He does not
mean that all sin is equally great, or that it is as serious
to break one commandment as to break all. Breaking
one commandment puts the offender in the class of transgressors. It also shows that he is indifferent to law, and
so to the will of God expressed in all the commandments,
and that it is but accident or fear or the absence of temptation that prevents him from breaking the other commandments. Most of all, it is evident that as love is the sum of
all the law, acting contrary to love is, in principle, breaking "the whole law."

We should be careful, then, as to our judgments, and
guard against all unfair discriminations, all narrow sus-
picions and class distinctions and race prejudices, for we

ourselves are to be judged. It is reassuring to know that
it is to be by "a law of liberty" and of love. Let us remember, however, that it is nevertheless by a law of justice, and "judgment is without mercy to him that hath
showed no mercy." So, as we hope to find that "mercy
glorieth against judgment," let love triumph in all our esti-
mates and judgments of our fellowmen. We shall not
then be guilty of holding the faith of our Lord Jesus Christ
"with respect of persons."

IV
FAITH AND WORKS
Ch. 2:14-26

14 What doth it profit, my brethren, if a man say he hath faith, but have not works? can that faith save him? 15 If a brother or sister be naked and in lack of daily food, 16 and one of you say unto them, Go in peace, be ye warmed and filled; and yet ye give them not the things needful to the body; what doth it profit? 17 Even so faith, if it have not works, is dead in itself. 18 Yea, a man will say, Thou hast faith, and I have works: show me thy faith apart from thy works, and I by my works will show thee my faith. 19 Thou believest that God is one; thou doest well: the demons also believe, and shudder. 20 But wilt thou know, O vain man, that faith apart from works is barren? 21 Was not Abraham our father justified by works, in that he offered up Isaac his son upon the altar? 22 Thou seest that faith wrought with his works, and by works was faith made perfect; 23 and the scripture was fulfilled which saith, And Abraham believed God, and it was reckoned unto him for righteousness; and he was called the friend of God. 24 Ye see that by works a man is justified, and not only by faith. 25 And in like manner was not also Rahab the harlot justified by works, in that she received the messengers, and sent them out another way? 26 For as the body apart from the spirit is dead, even so faith apart from works is dead.

It is right to say that James has no part in the popular discussion as to whether a man is saved by faith or saved by works. His concern is to prove that faith and works are inseparable. He never questions that faith is the instrument of salvation, but he insists that if faith is real it will manifest itself in works. Faith is trust and devotion and obedience and love; a "faith" which is mere assent to a creed is not worthy the name. A faith which does not produce works cannot save, it is "dead," it is "barren" —this is the truth which James seeks to establish in this famous section of his epistle.

He has been warning his readers against the folly of trying to hold faith in the Lord Jesus Christ and at the same time breaking the law of love and showing "respect of persons." He has insisted that this is impossible; real faith in Christ will manifest itself in love. He now proceeds to enlarge upon this vital truth and to insist that real faith will always be manifest in conduct which is consistent with the law and love of Christ.

James introduces the discussion by the question. "What doth it profit, my brethren, if a man say he hath faith, but have not works? can that faith save him?" The answer implied is that such faith cannot save; it is not true faith. James shows that it is not true by a comparison. He likens such dead faith to lifeless love: "If a brother or sister be naked and in lack of daily food, and one of you say unto them, Go in peace, be ye warmed and filled; and yet ye give them not the things needful to the body; what doth it profit?" What, indeed, is the use of charity like that? Love which confines itself to empty words, to cheap advice, to pious hopes, is not worthy the name. "Even so faith, if it have not works, is dead."

James further proves his point by an imaginary challenge: "Show me thy faith apart from thy works." That exposes the fallacy. Without works there is no possible way of proving that faith exists. Such faith is a phantom, a dream, a delusion. But, one who truly believes can say without pride yet in all confidence, "I by my works will show thee my faith."

To show further the vanity of a faith which consists in mere intellectual assent to truth, James takes a case in point. He turns to some Jew who plumes himself upon being orthodox, because he believes in the unity of God, and repeats daily the formula of his faith: "Thou believest that God is one; thou doest well; the demons also believe, and shudder." The demons are quite orthodox in their beliefs and probably more exact in their knowledge than most mortals; but while conscious of their deserved doom and of their rebellion against God, their knowledge only adds to their distress: they shudder. Thus, James concludes, "faith apart from works is barren."

On the other hand, real faith necessarily embodies itself in action. The faith of a true believer will be indicated and demonstrated by works. To establish this positive side of his argument James employs two examples. The first is naturally that of Abraham, "the father of the faithful." When he was subjected to the supreme test, when he was asked to offer up Isaac his son upon the altar, his faith was found to be genuine; it was no mere assent to a creed, it was a faith that "wrought with his works, and by works was faith made perfect." Abraham was shown to have a supreme confidence in God, a matchless submission to his will; he really "believed God, and it was reckoned unto him for righteousness; and he was called the friend of God." So it is by works that a man is shown to be a true believer, James declares, and not by a mere profession of faith.

The second illustration is that of Rahab. She also was shown by her works to be sincere in her faith. At the risk of her life she hid the spies who entered Jericho, and "sent them out another way." It is true that her faith was not perfect; she was guilty of falsehood and deception; yet her faith was remarkable, and it was genuine. A poor, sinful woman of Canaan, with little opportunity for knowledge, she had become convinced that the God of Israel was the living and true God, and as opportunity offered of serving him, she imperiled her life to defend his messengers. The result was that she was saved; she was honored as a heroine in the Hebrew annals; she became the ancestress of Jesus Christ. Such is the power of a living faith. On the other hand: "As the body apart from the spirit is dead, even so faith apart from works is dead."

The days of dead orthodoxy are not gone; there are many persons whose faith consists in the recital of creeds and in the defense of dogmas, many who need to be reminded that "faith apart from works is dead"; yet again, on the other hand, it is time for men to cease proposing the false alternatives of "creed or character," "belief or conduct," "doctrine or duty"; these supposed alternatives are inseparable as causes and effects, as roots and fruit. When creeds are living, when belief is sincere, when doctrine is truly accepted, then character and right conduct and the performance of duty are sure to result. A living faith does save.

V

CONTROL OF THE TONGUE

*1 Be not many of you teachers, my brethren, knowing
that we shall receive heavier judgment. 2 For in many
things we all stumble. If any stumbleth not in word, the
same is a perfect man, able to bridle the whole body also.
3 Now if we put the horses' bridles into their mouths that
they may obey us, we turn about their whole body also.
4 Behold, the ships also, though they are so great and are
driven by rough winds, are yet turned about by a very small
rudder, whither the impulse of the steersman willeth. 5 So
the tongue also is a little member, and boasteth great things.
Behold, how much wood is kindled by how small a fire!
6 And the tongue is a fire: the world of iniquity among our
members is the tongue, which defileth the whole body, and
setteth on fire the wheel of nature, and is set on fire by hell.
7 For every kind of beasts and birds, of creeping things
and things in the sea, is tamed, and hath been tamed by
mankind: 8 but the tongue can no man tame; it is a restless evil, it is full of deadly poison. 9 Therewith bless we
the Lord and Father; and therewith curse we men, who are
made after the likeness of God: 10 out of the same mouth
cometh forth blessing and cursing. My brethren, these
things ought not so to be. 11 Doth the fountain send forth
from the same opening sweet water and bitter? 12 can a
fig tree, my brethren, yield olives, or a vine figs? neither can
salt water yield sweet.*

In a previous passage of the epistle, James has exposed
the folly of imagining oneself to be religious while the
tongue is uncontrolled. It is natural, therefore, for him to
enlarge upon this theme, after setting forth the vanity of a
"faith" which expresses itself only in words and not in
works. Those most tempted to such self-deception and to

such dead orthodoxy are teachers of religious truth, and it is such, first of all, who are in the mind of the writer as he pens this searching passage on the sins of the tongue. It is hardly necessary to note that by "the tongue" James means the gift of speech. The whole paragraph abounds in figures and pictures. We see the horse held in by the bit, the ship turned by the touch of the pilot, the forest set aflame by the smallest spark, venomous beasts, fruitful trees, and gushing fountains. It is a striking instance of the vivid and picturesque style of the writer; but it suggests what to his mind was the importance and the power of human speech. While he dwells on the evil possibilities of the tongue, he nevertheless has in mind its possibilities for good. Thus when he warns his readers against too great eagerness to be teachers, it is on the ground that as such their responsibility is greater; but the responsibility is greater only because of the largeness of their opportunity and privilege. Of course the abuse of such privilege involves the greater guilt. "Be not many of you teachers, my brethren, knowing that we shall receive heavier judgment." Teachers of religious truth are sorely needed; theirs is the highest of callings; yet one should be diffident in assuming the task as he remembers that "in many things we all stumble." The right use of speech, the proper control of the tongue, James declares, is a proof of Christian maturity, whether in the case of a teacher or a hearer: "If any stumbleth not in word, the same is a perfect man, able to bridle the whole body also." This point he illustrates by his picture of the horse; in spite of its spirit and strength its whole body can be controlled by the one who controls the bit. The same point is illustrated by the ship: even though its size is so vast, and opposing storms are so fierce, still its course is easily determined by the one who holds the helm. These two pictures illustrate also another principle: they not only show how one who controls his tongue can control his whole being, but also that if the tongue is given control, it will imperil the entire life. The tongue is like the bit and like the rudder. "So the tongue also is a little member, and boasteth great things." It boasts. We were ready for the word "directs" or "controls" or "achieves," but the word "boasteth" is suggestive of evil and prepares us for the following description of perilous power.

As a single spark sets fire to the stately forest, so one malicious word may bring disaster to a life or a community. Thus James calls the tongue "a fire: the world of iniquity among our members . . . which defileth the whole body"; it sets ablaze the whole round of our existence and our being, and its destructive power is satanic: it "is set on fire by hell." The impossibility of bringing it under control is further emphasized by comparison with savage and venomous animals: "For every kind of beasts and birds, of creeping things and things in the sea, is tamed, and hath been tamed by mankind: but the tongue can no man tame." Of course James is not considering here what can be done by the grace and Spirit of God. He means that by nature the gift of speech is less commonly brought under control of man, than are the fiercest of the beasts about him. Like such beasts, the tongue is restless, unreliable, treacherous; like a serpent it is armed with venom, "it is full of deadly poison."

Last of all, James emphasizes the strange perversity and inconsistency with which men use the gift of speech. With the tongue, praises are offered to our heavenly Father, and with the same tongue, curses are pronounced upon his children whom he has created in his own image; "out of the same mouth cometh forth blessing and cursing." "My brethren, these things ought not so to be." The simplest objects in the world about us rebuke such a practice as unnatural: "Doth the fountain send forth from the same opening sweet water and bitter?" It is not unusual to find a spring the water of which is brackish and bitter, but who ever found such a spring which at the same time produced water which was sweet? "Can a fig tree, my brethren, yield olives, or a vine figs? neither can salt water yield sweet." These last figures contain not only a rebuke of the perverse and sinful abuse of speech; they also suggest the probable explanation of such an abuse. "The tree is known by its fruit," and "out of the abundance of the heart the mouth speaketh." An evil tongue is a sign of an evil nature. Unkind, bitter, impure speech suggests the need of a new birth; it is an indication that the speaker, whatever his position or profession, is not filled with the Spirit of God. His faith is dead, his religion is not true. The use of the tongue is a test of life. Unless controlled by the power of Christ, the gift of speech may prove a deadly peril to the soul.

VI
FALSE AND TRUE WISDOM

Ch. 3:13-18

13 Who is wise and understanding among you? let him show by his good life his works in meekness of wisdom. 14 But if ye have bitter jealousy and faction in your heart, glory not and lie not against the truth. 15 This wisdom is not a wisdom that cometh down from above, but is earthly, sensual, devilish. 16 For where jealousy and faction are, there is confusion and every vile deed. 17 But the wisdom that is from above is first pure, then peaceable, gentle, easy to be entreated, full of mercy and good fruits, without variance, without hypocrisy. 18 And the fruit of righteousness is sown in peace for them that make peace.

The churches addressed by James were troubled by the contentions of self-appointed teachers who were proud of boasted knowledge, who were fond of dispute, who were bitter in their discussions, who were more eager to defeat their opponents than to establish the truth. Having rebuked their evil use of the tongue, James suggests that the fault is due to their evil hearts, and that their vaunted wisdom, judged by its expression, is false and unreal. Unfortunately the persons described are not confined to the class of teachers or to the churches of the first century. The spirit here reproved is manifested today by many who profess to know Christ, and who claim, in their angry disputes, to be defending his cause.

"Who is wise and understanding among you?" James does not intend to suggest, by his question, that none were such, but rather to challenge those who had been loudest in their boasts. "Let him show by his good life his works in meekness of wisdom." This is a fair test. This is the

main point of the epistle. This is the modern demand for
reality in religion. Let faith be proved by deeds, let wisdom be shown by works.

In mentioning the test of "meekness," James does not
mean to advocate weakness, the two should never be associated. Only the strong, who are conscious of their power,
are truly meek; the insistence here is upon the modesty
which is the mark of true wisdom. "But if ye have bitter
jealousy and faction in your heart," if cruel envy and a
narrow party spirit are your motives, "glory not" even
though you are fighting on the right side, even though you
seem to have scored a victory, "and lie not against the
truth," for your spirit shows your boasted wisdom to be
false.

The character of this false "wisdom" is described as
being not "from above"; it does not have its source in
God. It is "earthly," bounded by earthly horizons, in accordance with earthly standards, identified with earthly
motives, plainly contradicting the claims of heavenly
knowledge and revealed truth; it is "sensual," by which is
meant not merely fleshly, but unspiritual, characterizing
only the "natural man" uninfluenced by the Spirit of God,
and so proving false all pretensions of divine enlightenment and superior knowledge; it is "devilish," it is one
with the spirit than animates demons. It may be employed in discussing religious truth, it may be displayed
in defending "orthodoxy," but it is evidently not inspired
by the Spirit of God; no matter what his intellectual attainments, no one should pride himself upon a wisdom which
is so closely allied with "the world, the flesh, and the devil."

The result of this false wisdom is described as being
utter "confusion" and evil of every kind; for heated de-
bates, proud display of learning, bitter sarcasm, lead only
to discord and separations; "for where jealousy and faction are, there is confusion and every vile deed."

In striking contrast, James describes "the wisdom that
is from above." It is "first" of all and supremely "pure,"

cleansed from all stain of selfishness and dedicated wholly to the service of God. It is "then peaceable"—not at the price of purity, not so as to compromise truth, not so as to countenance evil—yet not quarrelsome, not contentious, not desiring to dispute, but hungering for peace even if compelled to fight. It is "gentle," not always insisting upon its rights, considerate of others, characterized by "sweet reasonableness." It is "easy to be entreated," not stubborn, not refusing to do a thing because it has been suggested by another, submissive, tractable, conciliatory. It is "full of mercy and good fruits"; instead of envy and hatred it is characterized by compassion and love; instead of producing bitterness and confusion and wrath, its fruitage is helpfulness, and kindness, and joy, and enlarging life. It is "without variance," which probably means "without vacillation" or doubt or indecision or uncertainty, but with definiteness of conviction. It is "without hypocrisy," it needs none; it has nothing to hide, it makes no pretense; it is absolutely honest and sincere. Such is the heavenly "wisdom," the divine understanding which God gives to those who really trust in him. Those who are thus endowed, those who in contrast with the lovers of strife are makers of peace, those who really sow the seed of peace, are preparing no harvest of evil and distress, but the blessed and peaceful fruits of righteousness.

VII
WORLDLY LUSTS
Ch. 4:1-10

1 Whence come wars and whence come fightings among you? come they not hence, even of your pleasures that war in your members? 2 Ye lust, and have not: ye kill, and covet, and cannot obtain: ye fight and war; ye have not, because ye ask not. 3 Ye ask, and receive not, because ye ask amiss, that ye may spend it in your pleasures. 4 Ye adulteresses, know ye not that the friendship of the world is enmity with God? Whosoever therefore would be a friend of the world maketh himself an enemy of God. 5 Or think ye that the scripture speaketh in vain? Doth the spirit which he made to dwell in us long unto envying? 6 But he giveth more grace. Wherefore the scripture saith, God resisteth the proud, but giveth grace to the humble. 7 Be subject therefore unto God; but resist the devil, and he will flee from you. 8 Draw nigh to God, and he will draw nigh to you. Cleanse your hands, ye sinners; and purify your hearts, ye doubleminded. 9 Be afflicted, and mourn, and weep: let your laughter be turned to mourning, and your joy to heaviness. 10 Humble yourselves in the sight of the Lord, and he shall exalt you.

How can war be ended forever? How eagerly this question is being asked by a world in anguish, and what various replies are being made! James proposes a more profound question: What is the occasion of war? "Whence come wars and whence come fightings among you?" Only when the causes are removed will wars cease to devastate and destroy. These causes, James intimates, may be found in the selfishness of the human heart, in the desire for possessions and power, and in worldly lusts. It is probable that the primary reference in this paragraph is not to wars between nations, but to the strifes and factions in the Christian church which the writer has been rebuking. He has spoken of the abuse of the tongue and has exposed the false wisdom of the wrangling teachers; he now traces the evils to their source and shows the seriousness of their results. The latter is emphasized by the use of the words "wars" and "fightings" which are contrasted with the "peace" of true wisdom which the preceding verse has set forth. These "wars," whether between nations or individuals, are due to selfishness, or, as James says in addressing these professed Christians: "Come they not hence, even of your pleasures that war in your members?" By "pleasures" he means the love of sinful, sensuous, selfish gratifications. These "lusts" encamp in our bodily members; here first they make themselves felt, and these are the instruments they first employ. These "lusts," these unrestrained cravings, these covetous desires, may grow stronger even when not gratified, and may result in murder, at least in thought if not in act, in envy, in fighting and war: "Ye lust, and have not: ye kill, and covet, and cannot obtain: ye fight and war." Even prayer is resorted to as a means of securing the desired satisfaction: "Ye have not because ye ask not"; such a mere travesty upon prayer is of course unanswered. "Ye ask, and receive not, because ye ask amiss, that you may spend it in your pleasures"; such is a perversion of the true spirit of prayer which is submission to the will of God; here the desire is consciously opposed to his will. It is of course proper to pray for personal benefits, if these are innocent, and for material blessings if these are needed; but to ask for help in gratifying impure or sinful or selfish impulses is an impertinence and an insult to God.

In fact, it is our relation to God as professing Christians that suggests the more serious aspect of the issue of our "worldly lusts"; they not only lead us to fight and war against our fellowmen, but they make us disloyal to God. This disloyalty is expressed under the Old Testament

figure of "adultery": "Ye adulteresses, know ye not that
the friendship of the world is enmity with God?"   To
him we have sworn our allegiance and our fidelity; if then
our heart is given to "the world" of lust and greed and indulgence, we are faithless to our most solemn vows.   One
must choose between God and "the world" of selfish pleasures and sin; a preference for the latter is open hostility to
God: "Whosoever therefore would be a friend of the world
maketh himself an enemy of God."   The fault is all the
greater because of God's infinite love for us.   As a husband
can brook no rival for the affections of his wife, God is
jealous for the individual affection of his people.   Love
hungers for love.   Is it true then, of any of us, that our
affection is so alienated as to move God to envy; or that,
as some have translated the phrase, "the Spirit which he
made to dwell in us jealously yearns for the entire devotion
of the heart?"

"But he giveth more grace," that is, the very greatness
of his love leads him not to cast us off for our unfaithfulness, but to receive and to forgive us when we turn to him.
Yes, this infinite love enables him to realize how strong
are the attractions which draw us away, and to give us all
needed grace when we humbly look to him for help:
"God resisteth the proud, but giveth grace to the humble.
Be subject therefore unto God."   Do not presume upon
his goodness; do not weakly yield to temptation; do not
expect him to keep you from falling unless you are resolute
in your determination and are bravely fighting against sin.
All theories of Christian experience which suggest the inactivity of the human will, and prescribe mere submission
and dependence on the part of the believer, are dangerous.
"Resist the devil, and he will flee from you.   Draw nigh
to God, and he will draw nigh to you." Both actions and
attitudes are to be ours; neither is to be minimized nor
neglected.

So common is our unfaithfulness that we may well heed,
as directed to us, the solemn call to repentance with which

the paragraph is brought to a close: "Cleanse your hands, ye sinners; and purify your hearts, ye doubleminded"; let us separate ourselves from all sinful alliances, let us cease from all divided allegiance and devotion. "Be afflicted, and mourn, and weep": not because religion is a matter of gloom and sadness, but because we are too far tempted to miss its real joy by treating our sins lightly and failing to surrender our whole hearts to God. Some people have only enough religion to make them miserable. If we should renounce all that may be contrary to the will of God, if we should make him the center of our affections, we should know in all its fullness the joy of his salvation: "Humble yourselves in the sight of the Lord, and he shall exalt you."

VIII
CENSORIOUSNESS
Ch. 4:11-12

11 Speak not one against another, brethren. He that speaketh against a brother, or judgeth his brother, speaketh against the law, and judgeth the law: but if thou judgest the law, thou art not a doer of the law, but a judge. 12 One only is the lawgiver and judge, even he who is able to save and to destroy: but who art thou that judgest thy neighbor?

In reading these words, we are at once reminded of the Sermon on the Mount: "Judge not, that ye be not judged. . . . And why beholdest thou the mote that is in thy brother's eyes, but considerest not the beam that is in thine own eye?"; or we recall the Epistle to the Romans: "But thou, why dost thou judge thy brother? . . . for we shall all stand before the judgment-seat of God." But not only do they reflect the teachings of Jesus and of Paul; they are also vitally related to what has been said by James. He has rebuked the abuse of the tongue which is employed in criticizing our brethren; he has exposed the pride of false "wisdom" which leads us to form unjust judgments; he has rebuked the selfish desires which result in "wars" and contention and which make us untrue to God; he now warns us against censoriousness as usurping the place of God as lawgiver and judge.

"Speak not one against another." We cannot avoid forming opinions of our fellowmen, but these should not be unjust or unkind; and, whether good or bad, opinions need not always be expressed. It is the love of finding fault which James here rebukes. It is the same sin which is censured by Jesus and by Paul, but the condemnation is on different grounds. Jesus intimates the folly of finding fault with those who are probably much better than ourselves; Paul censures the presumption of correcting one who is not your servant and who must answer to the divine Master to whom he belongs; James argues that evil-speaking and censoriousness involve a breach of the law, an actual repudiation of the law: "He that speaketh against a brother, or judgeth his brother, speaketh against the law, and judgeth the law." Of course the law to which James refers is the law of love, "the royal law," "thou shalt love thy neighbor as thyself." One who is unkind in his criticisms not only breaks this law, but he condemns it as too high in its requirements or as unwise or unnecessary; he says in effect that he is superior to the law of love; he seems to argue that while it may be a good law for some people at some times, a superior person like himself cannot be bound by it, particularly in this imperfect world where some people need to be disciplined by his severe rebukes and punished by his stinging tongue. James intimates that, to say the least, it is better to keep the law of love than to try to find exceptions to its universal obligation. Most serious of all, such an attitude toward the law and toward other persons as is involved in censoriousness is invading the rights and prerogatives of God; he alone is the source of law, he alone is qualified to condemn men: "One only is the lawgiver and judge"; he allows no one to cancel his laws or to debate his decisions. The right is based upon his unique power; he "is able to save and to destroy"; he who can determine the fate of immortal souls is qualified to pronounce sentence upon them.

By way of contrast, James asks, "But who art thou that judgest thy neighbor?" What superior virtue, power, holiness, wisdom do you possess? A humble searching of our own hearts removes all eagerness to criticize and condemn others. "Love covereth a multitude of sins"; love "beareth all things"; "love suffereth long, and is kind."

IX
SELF–CONFIDENCE
Ch. 4:13-17

> *13 Come now, ye that say, To-day or to-morrow we will go into this city, and spend a year there, and trade, and get gain: 14 whereas ye know not what shall be on the morrow. What is your life? For ye are a vapor that appeareth for a little time, and then vanisheth away. 15 For that ye ought to say, If the Lord will, we shall both live, and do this or that. 16 But now ye glory in your vauntings: all such glorying is evil. 17 To him therefore that knoweth to do good, and doeth it not, to him it is sin.*

James has just condemned the selfish, worldly spirit which manifests itself in "wars and fightings," and also the presumption which takes the place of God in pronouncing judgment upon our fellowmen. These are closely related to the false confidence in which we make plans for the future with no thought of God. As he now turns to rebuke such godless conceit, James rehearses the imaginary words of certain Jewish traders who are perfecting their schemes for a coming year: "Come now, ye that say, To-day or to-morrow we will go into this city, and spend a year there, and trade, and get gain." Every step is detailed with absolute assurance, no suggestion is made of divine providence, no thought is entertained as to the will of God. "To-day or to-morrow" are regarded as alike completely within their power; the journey to the city selected is certain to be safe; the year is quite at their disposal; neither sickness nor disaster can possibly come; the business venture is sure to be prosperous; such seem to be the thoughts of these confident merchants, and their spirit is too commonly reflected by the professed followers of Christ. We are all tempted to regard the future with presumptuous assurance. We all need to be reminded of the words of James: "Whereas ye know not what shall be on the morrow. What is your life? For ye are a vapor that appeareth for a little time, and then vanisheth away." Not that it is wrong to make plans, not that it is wrong to engage in business, not that it is wrong to expect "gain"; but the uncertain tenure of life, the mystery of the future, the knowledge that God has for each of us a purpose and a plan, should make us conscious of our dependence upon him, and eager to know and to do his will: "For that ye ought to say, If the Lord will, we shall both live, and do this or that." James does not mean that the expressions, "Please God" or "The Lord willing," should continually be on our lips; that might be mere formalism or cant; but the truth of God's providence, the belief that life and its blessings are his gifts, the reverent conviction that the future is wholly within his power, should so mold all our thinking that self-confidence and presumption would be impossible. On the contrary, to forget God, to plan with no thought of him, to regard the future with boastful assurance, is not only foolish, it is wicked: "But now ye glory in your vauntings; all such glorying is evil." James concludes the paragraph by referring to a principle of wide scope and great importance: "To him therefore that knoweth to do good, and doeth it not, to him it is sin." It is not only wrong to perform an act which we know to be contrary to the will of God, or about which we are uncertain; it is also wrong to fail to do what we know to be the will of God. It does not make life burdensome or gloomy, but it fills it with joy and satisfaction, when in all its choices and crises we can say from the heart: "If the Lord will, we shall both live, and do this or that." Surely "in his will is our peace."

X
THE DOOM
OF THE OPPRESSOR
Ch. 5:1-6

1 Come now, ye rich, weep and howl for your miseries that are coming upon you. 2 Your riches are corrupted, and your garments are moth-eaten. 3 Your gold and your silver are rusted; and their rust shall be for a testimony against you, and shall eat your flesh as fire. Ye have laid up your treasure in the last days. 4 Behold, the hire of the laborers who mowed your fields, which is of you kept back by fraud, crieth out: and the cries of them that reaped have entered into the ears of the Lord of Sabaoth. 5 Ye have lived delicately on the earth, and taken your pleasure; ye have nourished your hearts in a day of slaughter. 6 Ye have condemned, ye have killed the righteous one; he doth not resist you.

It is easy to criticize the rich, and in some quarters it is always popular to denounce men of wealth. It must be remembered, however, that no sin is involved in the possession of money, and that there is no virtue in being poor. Wealth has peculiar temptations and grave responsibilities; yet not all rich persons are to be condemned or to be under suspicion. If poverty is voluntarily assumed, it should be for some good purpose. As to riches, two questions should be asked: How are they secured? How are they used? The persons whom James condemned were guilty on both these counts. They may have been Christians, or, more probably, unconverted Jews; beyond doubt they belonged to a class with which we are all familiar today. They had amassed their wealth by fraud and cruelty; they were spending it in selfish luxury.

Upon such, James pronounces a solemn doom, as he warns them that the coming of Christ may be near: "Come now, ye rich, weep and howl for your miseries that are coming upon you." Their folly appears in the heaping together of unused wealth; if it consists of products of the earth, it will corrupt; if in garments, they will be eaten by moths; if in precious metals, they will tarnish and rust; its rapid decay is a fit symbol of the swift destruction of its owners. Their folly is seen further in the fact that their struggle for wealth is made under the shadow of approaching doom: "Ye have laid up your treasure in the last days." The possibility that the return of Christ might be near, like the fact of the brevity and uncertainty of life, should be a warning against the worldly spirit which in the previous paragraph led to presumptuous plans for the future, and which here is expressed in amassing wealth which the owners never can enjoy.

These rich men, however, are guilty not only of folly but also of sin. Their wealth has been secured by injustice: "Behold, the hire of the laborers who mowed your fields, which is of you kept back by fraud, crieth out." This is the crime of oppressors in all ages, refusing a fair wage, keeping back what has been earned by the employees whose toil has secured the wealth the employers enjoy. This, supremely, occasions "the social question." Such injustice is related to other forms of cruelty; "Ye have condemned, ye have killed the righteous one; he doth not resist you." It was easy for the wealthy to control the processes of law for condemning and defrauding the helpless poor; the latter were being "killed" not necessarily with the sword, but by lack of food and improper conditions of labor and by the crushing monotony of ceaseless toil; but the silent appeal of their patient helplessness was unheeded. The rich oppressors were deaf to all entreaties. They were too much occupied in their own enjoyments to know the very conditions which existed. Their sin consisted not only in the injustice by which their wealth was secured, but in the prodigal luxury in which it was spent: "Ye have lived delicately on the earth, and taken your pleasure." There was One, however, who heard the moaning of the helpless sufferers: their cries "have entered into the ears of the Lord of Sabaoth." The guilty oppressors are like sheep, fattening themselves for slaughter; the Lord of Hosts soon will lay bare his arm. Doom is certain.

XI

PATIENCE IN SUFFERING

Ch. 5:7-11

7 Be patient therefore, brethren, until the coming of the Lord. Behold, the husbandman waiteth for the precious fruit of the earth, being patient over it, until it receive the early and latter rain. 8 Be ye also patient; establish your hearts: for the coming of the Lord is at hand. 9 Murmur not, brethren, one against another, that ye be not judged: behold, the judge standeth before the doors. 10 Take, brethren, for an example of suffering and of patience, the prophets who spake in the name of the Lord. 11 Behold, we call them blessed that endured: ye have heard of the patience of Job, and have seen the end of the Lord, how that the Lord is full of pity, and merciful.

The suffering by which the readers were being tried was caused by cruel oppression, especially on the part of employers. Under these conditions, employees are tempted to words and deeds unworthy of Christians. While every lawful effort should be made to better conditions and to secure justice for themselves and others, nevertheless, under even the most cruel treatment, believers must manifest a spirit of patient endurance.

The motive to which James appeals is the expectation of the speedy return of Christ: "Be patient therefore, brethren, until the coming of the Lord." Many wrongs may be righted, many social customs may be improved, before the visible reappearing of the Savior, but his coming is "the blessed hope," both for the church and the world; then justice will be meted out to oppressor and oppressed; then will begin an age of righteousness and peace.

The illustration suggested by the writer is that of a

farmer who, after planting the seed, waits for the early rain in the fall and the "latter rain" in the spring and so for the ripened harvest: "Be ye also patient; establish your hearts: for the coming of the Lord is at hand." Meanwhile, their grievous sufferings must not make them fretful and complaining and unforgiving in their relations with fellow Christians; at his coming the Lord will bring judgment upon them as well as vengeance upon their enemies. They might also be encouraged by the example of ancient prophets and saints who testified and suffered in the name of the Lord: "Behold, we call them blessed that endured." They are reminded in particular of Job; he was not very patient, if by patience we mean freedom from complaint and irritation and anger, but here the thought is of steadfast "endurance," the quality of invincible faith in God; this Job possessed, and his whole life story is an illustration of how, in the end, the Lord always shows his pity and mercy and vindicates his justice and his love toward those that trust and "wait for" him.

XII
PROFANITY
Ch. 5:12

> 12 But above all things, my brethren, swear not, neither
> by the heaven, nor by the earth, nor by any other oath:
> but let your yea be yea, and your nay, nay; that ye fall not
> under judgment.

Profane swearing is one of the worst and most senseless
of sins; yet, possibly it is as prevalent today as at any time
since James wrote these lines. It would be interesting to
study the philosophy or the psychology of swearing. The
practice may spring from a desire for emphasis, particularly when one is provoked and seeks to express disap-
proval and disgust. This explanation may account for
the connection in which these words are found. James
has just referred to the cruel oppression of the rich and
powerful, and to their unjust treatment of Christians; he
now insists that under even such provocation one is not
to take the name of the Lord, our God, in vain, or to dis-
obey the strict injunction of Jesus Christ: "Swear not at
all." The exact words of our Lord were undoubtedly in
mind and were quoted in part by James. The question has
often been raised whether the reference here includes
the prohibition of oaths in courts of law; it would seem,
from the practice of Paul, of Jesus before his judges, of the
early church, and of the Old Testament requirements,
that legal oaths are not here in mind; however, it must be
admitted that even such swearing is a concession to the
dishonesty and incredulity of men—it would not be
necessary in an ideal society; yet, as its aim is to secure
veracity and to defend truth, its practice may hasten the
day when "yea" and "nay" will suffice to establish legal

testimony. Surely the use of the divine name to express irritation and anger or to strengthen ordinary affirmation of speech, is not only frivolous and foolish, but irreverent and sinful; it brings one "under judgment." It can usually be corrected by that which underlies the keeping of all law, namely, truer love to God and to men.

XIII
PRAYER FOR THE SICK
Ch. 5:13-18

13 Is any among you suffering? let him pray. Is any cheerful? let him sing praise. 14 Is any among you sick? let him call for the elders of the church; and let them pray over him, anointing him with oil in the name of the Lord: 15 and the prayer of faith shall save him that is sick, and the Lord shall raise him up; and if he have committed sins, it shall be forgiven him. 16 Confess therefore your sins one to another, and pray one for another, that ye may be healed. The supplication of a righteous man availeth much in its working. 17 Elijah was a man of like passions with us, and he prayed fervently that it might not rain; and it rained not on the earth for three years and six months. 18 And he prayed again; and the heaven gave rain, and the earth brought forth her fruit.

This difficult but helpful passage is introduced with a possible reference to the verse which precedes; not profanity but prayer and praise are the proper expressions of emotion: "Is any among you suffering," in body or mind or estate? "let him pray. Is any cheerful? let him sing praise." Worship which consists in prayer and praise, worship, whether in private or public, is the channel by which our excited feelings are to be given an outlet. Whenever the mind is violently agitated, the most rational relief will be found in an act of worship; above all, in times of distress our recourse should be to prayer.

One of the most common occasions of distress is that of sickness. James mentions this as a specific case in which believers are to seek relief in prayer, and his words form the famous passage on "prayer and bodily healing": "Is any among you sick? let him call for the elders of the church; and let them pray over him, anointing him with oil in the name of the Lord: and the prayer of faith shall save him that is sick, and the Lord shall raise him up; and if he have committed sins, it shall be forgiven him." In reference to a passage so much debated, it would be foolish to speak with dogmatic assurance. A few suggestions, however, may be of help.

a. The use of oil as a medicine, and its application in cases of disease, has been familiar in all ages; and it is a sufficiently satisfactory interpretation of these verses to say that they prescribe, in the case of bodily sickness, prayer and the use of simple remedies.

b. It may be, however, that sending for "elders" instead of a "beloved physician," and the anointing with oil "in the name of the Lord," point to the regulated exercise of the miraculous "gift of healing," which undoubtedly was granted to the early church, but which, like the gifts of "tongues," and "prophecy" and "immunity from deadly poisons," no longer exists.

c. The emphasis is on "the prayer of faith," and possibly the "oil" is a symbol of the Holy Spirit, by whom the cure was to be effected; the faith of the sufferer would be strengthened by the use of the familiar remedy, and, as his sins seem to have been connected with the cause of his disease, he would be reminded of the cleansing and healing power of the Spirit of God.

d. There is no reference here to "extreme unction"; this is designed to prepare the soul for death; the anointing by "the elders" was intended to restore the body to health.

e. Here the confession of sins was not to a priest or to an elder alone, but to any fellow Christian: "Confess therefore your sins one to another, and pray one for another, that ye may be healed."

f. In all modern uses of the passage, care should be taken to distinguish between "the prayer of faith," and such beliefs and practices as are associated with "Christian Science," "Mental Healing," or "Faith Healing."

"Christian Science" is in conflict with physical science in its views of matter, of pain, of disease, and of death; it contradicts Christianity in denying the incarnation, the death, and the resurrection of Jesus Christ. "Mental Healing" may be quite independent of any religious belief, or on the other hand it may be united with Christian faith; but it operates according to the scientific law of "the effect of mind upon matter." Its greatest failures are due to neglecting the complementary principle of "the effect of matter upon mind." "Faith Healing" forbids the use of all physical means, and any employment of physical science in the treatment of disease. Its advocates are devout and sincere and intelligent Christians. It is a mistake to confuse them with "Christian Scientists," or "Mental Healers." Their errors consist in the belief that the use of natural means is dishonoring to God; in their exclusive claim of "spiritual healing," when in reality a cure effected by a physician or surgeon might as truly be "spiritual," accomplished by the power and guidance of the Spirit of God; in their oblivion to the fact that the cures in which they rejoice are effected by the use of means, namely, by means of mental suggestion made by their prayers and their anointings.

g. "The prayer of faith" is offered in the assurance that God can work with or without means known to man, but in the belief that all wise remedies should be employed, while the trust is in God, and while the will is submissive to the will of God. The faith is not in the means, but in God who works through the means. In the whole passage the emphasis is upon the need of faith, and upon the power of believing prayer. Thus the paragraph closes with the example of Elijah, at whose request rain was given or withheld. The fact is emphasized that he was "a man of like passions with us" and that we need not wait until we become perfect before we pray; yet his was a prayer of intense earnestness and triumphant faith. In applying the truth of this paragraph, we should guard against the employment of prayer without means, and also of means without prayer. We should remember that the other equally famous passage of this epistle insists that "faith apart from works is dead."

XIV
SAVING SOULS
Ch. 5:19-20

*19 My brethren, if any among you err from the truth,
and one convert him; 20 let him know, that he who con-
verteth a sinner from the error of his way shall save a soul
from death, and shall cover a multitude of sins.*

The last message of the epistle is vitally related to the
message which precedes. There we were concerned with
bodily healing, but also with the forgiveness of the sins
to which the sickness may have been due; here we are
encouraged to have a part in the healing of souls; but while
in the former case we were concerned with those who felt
their need, here we are encouraged to seek for those who
may be ignorant of their danger or indifferent to their
peril. The case is that of one who has gone astray: he
has erred "from the truth," not so much in the matter of
belief as of practice. To bring him back again to the right
path will "save a soul from death," and "cover a multitude
of sins." In such saving work, every follower of Christ
may be engaged. Surely we shall need to resort anew, as
in the cases of physical healing, to the "prayer of faith";
surely there must be in our own religious experiences that
reality upon which the epistle everywhere insists; surely,
we must seek "the wisdom that is from above," which is
"first pure, then peaceable, gentle, easy to be entreated,
full of mercy and good fruits, without variance, without
hypocrisy."

THE FIRST EPISTLE OF PETER

THE FIRST EPISTLE
OF PETER

Who does not know Simon Peter, and who has not found in him a kindred spirit? Brave, impulsive, confident, unstable, affectionate Peter! Of all the apostles, his career is most vivid in memory, his character is most human and most real.

It is easy to imagine his early life as a fisherman of Galilee, or to picture his interest in the preaching of the Baptist and his first meeting with Jesus, or to recall how he left his boat and his nets to become a fisher of men, how he entered the inner circle of his Master's friends and became the leader and spokesman for the Twelve. It is not difficult to sketch the scenes where he attempts to walk on the water, where he boldly confesses his faith in Christ, where he speaks bewildered by the glory of the transfiguration, where he protests his deathless love, where he sleeps in the Garden and awakes to attempt the rash defense of his Lord whom he then forsakes and with an oath denies. We see him weeping in deep penitence, running to the empty tomb, meeting the risen Savior, and later receiving a new commission in the morning twilight by the lake. How distinctly we remember him as he speaks to the trembling multitudes at Pentecost, heals the lame man at the Beautiful Gate, boldly faces the Jewish rulers, meets Cornelius and opens the church to Gentile believers, is imprisoned by Herod and delivered by the angel, bravely defends Christian liberty in the council at Jerusalem and denies it in principle by his behavior at Antioch.

It is not difficult even to accept the shadowy legends which concern his later life, and to imagine that he preached at Rome, that as he attempted to escape the rising storm of persecution he met his Master at the city gate and asked him whither he was going (*"Domine, quo vadis"*), and received the reply, "I go to Rome, there to be crucified once more," that he turned back to suffer as the Master had, only with his head downward that he might endure more anguish and more shame than his Lord.

It may require more effort, however, to picture Peter as a prominent figure in the world of literature, and to remember that this "unlettered layman," as the rulers regarded him, was one of the authors of the New Testament, one of the immortals among the writers of the Christian era, and to recall the fact that his abiding influence is linked to the two epistles which bear his name.

The first of these letters was written to Christians dwelling in portions of what is now known as Asia Minor. Many of these readers were converts from Judaism, and Peter writes with continual reference to the Old Testament; but large numbers were Gentiles, and frequent mention is made of their former mode of life. More important is the fact that all these converts were in the midst of cruel hardships and temptations. They were not suffering from a persecution instituted by the state, but from social ostracism, and from the enmity of fanatical Jews and hostile pagans. They were compelled to endure slander, violence, hatred, suspicion, loss of goods, worldly ruin. To those in distress and trials so bitter and fiery, Peter writes to give counsel and comfort, to strengthen faith and to inspire courage.

This is an epistle of hope. It points the believer to the blessed issues of trial, and teaches him to regard present darkness in the light of a future which is radiant with the visible glory of Christ.

It is composed of three great sections which emphasize successively the privileges, the duties, and the trials of the readers. The presentation is intensely practical. The epistle is in substance a threefold series of earnest exhortations. It may be outlined as follows:

1. The Greeting *I Peter 1:1-2*
2. The Thanksgiving *Ch. 1:3-12*
3. Exhortations in View of Special Privileges *Chs. 1:13 to 2:10*
    a. Holiness *Ch. 1:13-21*
    b. Brotherly Love *Ch. 1:22-25*
    c. Growth as the People of God *Ch. 2:1-10*
4. Exhortations in View of Special Relations *Chs. 2:11 to 4:11*
    a. Sojourners *Ch. 2:11-12*
    b. Citizens *Ch. 2:13-17*
    c. Servants *Ch. 2:18-25*
    d. Wives and Husbands *Ch. 3:1-7*
    e. Innocent Sufferers *Ch. 3:8-22*
    f. Opposed by Sinners *Ch. 4:1-6*
    g. Expecting the Coming of Christ *Ch. 4:7-11*
5. Exhortations in View of Special Trials *Chs. 4:12 to 5:11*
    a. Steadfastness *Ch. 4:12-19*
    b. Fidelity *Ch. 5:1-4*
    c. Humility, Trust, Vigilance, and Constancy *Ch. 5:5-11*
6. The Conclusion *Ch. 5:12-14*
    a. The Bearer and Purpose of the Letter *Ch. 5:12*
    b. The Salutation and Benediction *Ch. 5:13-14*

I

THE GREETING
I Peter 1:1-2

1 Peter, an apostle of Jesus Christ, to the elect who are sojourners of the Dispersion in Pontus, Galatia, Cappadocia, Asia, and Bithynia, 2 according to the foreknowledge of God the Father, in sanctification of the Spirit, unto obedience and sprinkling of the blood of Jesus Christ: Grace to you and peace be multiplied.

One need not feel deeply concerned in the debate as to whether the Christian converts addressed by Peter were Gentiles, or, as is quite probable, Jews by birth. What does thrill us is the belief that the blessings attributed to them belong to us, if we belong to Christ. These "sojourners of the Dispersion" in various provinces of modern Asia Minor, are called "elect," a term which was used to describe all believers; they were the chosen people of God, the special objects of his mercy and love, and this election was "according to the foreknowledge of God the Father," and due therefore to his deliberate purpose. The very sphere of their new life was "sanctification." The Holy Spirit set them apart from the world for the service of God and imparted to them his holiness. The purpose was that they should obey Christ and become partakers of all the benefits secured by his death. For these believers Peter voices the prayer: "Grace to you and peace be multiplied."

So it is true of all Christians; wherever they may be scattered abroad throughout the earth, they form one race, in virtue of a new and divine birth; they are "sojourners," "pilgrims," and "strangers," whose citizenship is in heaven, their real home. They owe all that they are to the providence and provision of God who sanctifies them by his

Spirit, who saves them by the work of his Son. Thus, in the opening words of this epistle, Peter sets forth its three great truths, and indicates its contents; the first section deals with the sanctification of the Spirit, the second emphasizes the atoning death of the Son, the last concerns the providence of the Father. Thus, too, he intimates that the salvation secured by the Father, Son, and Spirit, involves the free obedience of the human will and the offering of devoted service. Therefore as Christians, chosen by the Father, sanctified by the Spirit, redeemed by the Son, we are to remember with humble gratitude that for all we have we are indebted to the mercy of God, in all that we are we should depend upon the sanctifying influence of his Spirit, in all that we do we should seek to glorify his Son. Then we, too, may expect that in our experience grace and peace will "be multiplied."

II
THE THANKSGIVING
Ch. 1:3-12

3 Blessed be the God and Father of our Lord Jesus Christ, who according to his great mercy begat us again unto a living hope by the resurrection of Jesus Christ from the dead, 4 unto an inheritance incorruptible, and undefiled, and that fadeth not away, reserved in heaven for you, 5 who by the power of God are guarded through faith unto a salvation ready to be revealed in the last time. 6 Wherein ye greatly rejoice, though now for a little while, if need be, ye have been put to grief in manifold trials, 7 that the proof of your faith, being more precious than gold that perisheth though it is proved by fire, may be found unto praise and glory and honor at the revelation of Jesus Christ: 8 whom not having seen ye love; on whom, though now ye see him not, yet believing, ye rejoice greatly with joy unspeakable and full of glory: 9 receiving the end of your faith, even the salvation of your souls. 10 Concerning which salvation the prophets sought and searched diligently, who prophesied of the grace that should come unto you: 11 searching what time or what manner of time the Spirit of Christ which was in them did point unto, when it testified beforehand the sufferings of Christ, and the glories that should follow them. 12 To whom it was revealed, that not unto themselves, but unto you, did they minister these things, which now have been announced unto you through them that preached the gospel unto you by the Holy Spirit sent forth from heaven; which things angels desire to look into.

As in most Jewish letters, the address is followed by a blessing. In the former, Peter has shown that our salvation is secured by Father, Son, and Holy Spirit; he now returns thanks for this salvation as certain to be perfected in the future, as giving courage in the present, as having been predicted in the past. In pointing his readers to the future, Peter strikes the keynote of his epistle. It is expressed in the word "hope": "Blessed be the God and Father of our Lord Jesus Christ, who according to his great mercy begat us again unto a living hope." This hope, which is mentioned as the first result of our new birth, is defined as "living," not only in contrast with the deceitful and perishing hopes of earth, not only because its object is "eternal life," but because it is based upon "the resurrection of Jesus Christ from the dead." This truth of the resurrection holds a prominent place in the writings of Peter. He remembers the transforming power of the event in his own experience. He mentions it here as the very source of the new life of hope imparted to the believer by the grace of God. The object of this hope, the final blessedness of this life, is defined as being an "inheritance," an estate one is to receive from the Father in virtue of the "new birth." This inheritance is "incorruptible," it has no seeds of decay, it cannot perish; it is "undefiled," free from all stain of sin; it "fadeth not away," but is like the unwithering flowers of Paradise; it is "reserved in heaven," kept absolutely secure for those who are being kept for it; the latter are being "guarded," kept as in a garrison, "by the power of God," in view of their faith in him. From the assaults of trial and distress and temptation the besieged soul will soon be delivered. This salvation, this object of hope, this other aspect of the "inheritance," is "ready to be revealed." This revelation will be "in the last time," at the very end of the present age, at "the revelation of Jesus Christ," an event which, to the mind of the writer, might possibly be near.

For the present, the readers were subjected to manifold trials; as the letter shows, they were suffering from hatred, suspicion, violence, slander, and cruel persecution; nevertheless, in view of their coming "salvation," they were able to rejoice. Their distresses were but "for a little while";

they were part of the mysterious plan and providence of God; from them blessings would issue. These trials were tests of their faith; by them it was being refined and assayed, like gold; gold perishes at last, even though it can withstand the test of fire; their faith tested and purified would bring to them "praise and glory and honor" when Christ, their Savior, appeared. They were looking and longing for his return; though they had never seen him, they loved him; though his appearing was delayed, yet believing in him and expecting his coming, they were able to rejoice with a joy no tongue could express, a joy which was radiant with the glory of his return. So real was their faith that they already anticipated and were receiving the fulfillment of their hope, the joy of their inheritance, the "salvation" of their souls.

This salvation, wrought out by Christ, secured by his death and resurrection, was so marvelous in its character that believers might well rejoice in its possession. It had been the object of deepest concern and wonder to inspired writers. The latter had "sought and searched diligently" to find the exact time and the character of the time to which the Spirit of Christ, who guided them, was pointing "when it testified beforehand the sufferings" which were appointed for Christ "and the glories that should follow them." It was revealed to them that their predictions related to a future age, even that in which the readers of this epistle were living, one in which had taken place the events which were proclaimed in the gospel. This good news of salvation assured them that as they were now partakers of the sufferings of Christ, so too they should be of his "glories," which, predicted by prophets or proclaimed by apostles, were so great, so marvelous that the angels gazed upon them in eagerness and holy wonder.

III
EXHORTATIONS IN VIEW
OF SPECIAL PRIVILEGES
Chs. 1:13 to 2:10

a. Exhortation to Holiness   Ch. 1:13-21

13 Wherefore girding up the loins of your mind, be so-
ber and set your hope perfectly on the grace that is to be
brought unto you at the revelation of Jesus Christ; 14 as
children of obedience, not fashioning yourselves according
to your former lusts in the time of *your ignorance: 15 but*
like as he who called you is holy, be ye yourselves also holy
in all manner of living; 16 because it is written, Ye shall
be holy; for I am holy. 17 And if ye call on him as Father,
who without respect of persons judgeth according to each
man's work, pass the time of your sojourning in fear: 18
knowing that ye were redeemed, not with corruptible
things, with silver or gold, from your vain manner of life
handed down from your fathers; 19 but with precious
blood, as of a lamb without blemish and without spot, even
the blood *of Christ: 20 who was foreknown indeed be-*
fore the foundation of the world, but was manifested at the
end of the times for your sake, 21 who through him are be-
lievers in God, that raised him from the dead, and gave
him glory; so that your faith and hope might be in God.

Having given thanks to God for the wonderful salvation to be revealed in all fullness at the second coming of
Christ, Peter now urges his readers to conduct which is in
accord with their high privileges and glorious destiny. The
three chief exhortations are to holiness, to love, and to
growth. He introduces the first of these by suggesting the
animating principle of hope. "Wherefore . . . hope,"
is the substance of the first verse of the paragraph; "be

ye . . . holy," is the sum of the verses which remain.
"Wherefore," that is, in view of the deliverance from distresses and the heavenly inheritance which will be theirs
when Christ appears; "girding up the loins of your mind,"
as an Oriental would prepare himself for special effort by
gathering closely about him his loosely flowing robes, so
the mind of the Christian must be unhampered by sinful,
selfish, unbelieving thoughts; "be sober," or "being sober,"
that is "self-controlled," guarding against all fanatical and
foolish excitement, "set your hope perfectly on the grace
that is to be brought unto you at the revelation of Jesus
Christ."   At this present day, there is need for similar
caution in connection with the blessed hope which centers
in the return of Christ; first, there is still danger that the
hope may be neglected because the mind is hampered by
worldly, sinful distractions; second, there is a danger lest
it be associated with wild and fanatical vagaries; third, because of long delay and abundant discouragements, the
hope grows faint, it is not "set . . . perfectly," it does
not continue until the end.

Hope is mentioned, however, only as the motive to holiness.   The latter is the supreme thought of the paragraph.
This holiness is described negatively by a reference to the
former life of the readers, and positively by a reference
to the holiness of God.   "As children" who are such because of "obedience" to the divine call, and as those whose
whole purpose of life is to obey, they are exhorted no
longer to conform their acts and habits to the mode of
life which, before they knew Christ, was molded by selfish
and sinful desires.   "But like as he who called you is holy,
be ye yourselves also holy."   The root idea of holiness is
that of "separation," of dedication, particularly to the
service of God; it came, therefore, to denote the moral
character belonging to God himself.   The mention of this
as the standard for Christian living is inspiring.   If God
commands us to be holy, we can rest assured that he is
ready to give us needed grace, and even though in this

present time we fail to attain the divine ideal, we are thus encouraged to believe that perfect holiness is to be ours when Christ appears; it is part of our "inheritance."

Two special reasons are assigned for obeying this command: first, the fact that God is not only our Father but our Judge. He is loving, but he is also just, and can allow no sin in his children; therefore, we should spend the brief time of our "sojourning" here, before we go to his heavenly home, "in reverence and holy awe." The second reason is the fact that our ransom from the power of sin has been secured at so great cost, "even the blood of Christ"; it ever had been the divine purpose that he should be our Redeemer, and now after long ages of waiting he has appeared and finished his atoning work, has been raised from the dead, and has been exalted to the place of supreme power; through him we know God, on him our "faith and hope" are based.

b. Exhortation to Brotherly Love   Ch. 1:22-25

22 Seeing ye have purified your souls in your obedience to the truth unto unfeigned love of the brethren, love one another from the heart fervently: 23 having been begotten again, not of corruptible seed, but of incorruptible, through the word of God, which liveth and abideth. 24 For,

All flesh is as grass,
And all the glory thereof as the flower of grass.
The grass withereth, and the flower falleth:
25 But the word of the Lord abideth for ever.
And this is the word of good tidings which was preached unto you.

The new life of holiness, made possible by the redemption of Christ, is now made the basis of an exhortation to mutual love between believers. In fact, such love is suggested as the very object and purpose of that purification of soul which results from obedience to the revealed will of God. "Seeing ye have purified your souls"; this process was begun when the truth concerning Christ was first accepted, it has been continued in "obedience to the truth" and has its issue and goal in "unfeigned love of the brethren"; therefore, develop, cultivate, manifest this affection: "love one another from the heart fervently."

This love is natural, for Christians share a common life; all have one Father, and the spirit of Sonship should be the spirit of brotherhood. This love should be abiding, for the new life from which it springs is eternal, it comes from "incorruptible seed," communicated by means of the living message of salvation; for we have been "begotten again, not of corruptible seed, but of incorruptible, through the word of God which liveth and abideth." Mere natural, human love might wither and fade, but the affection of those whose new life has come through accepting the changeless, deathless truths of the gospel, will flourish and never fail; "all flesh is as grass, . . . but the word of the Lord abideth for ever."

Such love was needed by those early Christians, amid the withering heat of persecution and pain; such love is needed today where sorrows cast their shadows and where the night of grief and doubt deepens; it is the fragrant expression of the life of faith, it is the flower and the fruit of "the good tidings" concerning Christ.

c. Exhortation to Growth as the People of God
Ch. 2:1-10

1 Putting away therefore all wickedness, and all guile, and hypocrisies, and envies, and all evil speakings, 2 as newborn babes, long for the spiritual milk which is without guile, that ye may grow thereby unto salvation; 3 if ye have tasted that the Lord is gracious: 4 unto whom coming, a living stone, rejected indeed of men, but with God elect, precious, 5 ye also, as living stones, are built up a spiritual house, to be a holy priesthood, to offer up spiritual sacrifices, acceptable to God through Jesus Christ. 6 Because it is contained in scripture,

Behold, I lay in Zion a chief corner stone, elect, precious:
And he that believeth on him shall not be put to shame.

7 *For you therefore that believe is the preciousness: but for*
such as disbelieve,
> *The stone which the builders rejected,*
> *The same was made the head of the corner;*
8 *and,*
> *A stone of stumbling, and a rock of offence;*
for they stumble at the word, being disobedient: where-
unto also they were appointed. 9 But ye are an elect race,
a royal priesthood, a holy nation, a people for God's *own*
possession, that ye may show forth the excellencies of him
who called you out of darkness into his marvellous light:
10 who in time past were no people, but now are the people
of God: who had not obtained mercy, but now have ob-
tained mercy.

Having reminded his readers of the new life communicated to them through the gospel and by faith in Christ,
Peter next urges them to secure such growth and development as will fit them for service as the people of God. The
figures of speech are vivid and change with bewildering
rapidity; most of them are taken from the Old Testament,
and together they form almost a mosaic of quotations. At
first Christians are regarded as children, then as a temple,
and then as a priesthood, and then as the true "Israel of
God."

"As newborn babes, long for the spiritual milk . . . ,
that ye may grow thereby." The suggestion of spiritual
infancy is not intended here as a rebuke, but rather as an
encouragement to seek for the growth which all partakers
of the new life need. Negatively, this growth will be
secured by repressing all those motions and habits which
belong to the old life of sin, particularly such as are opposed to the brotherly love in which the new birth has
been shown to have its first and highest expression: "Putting away therefore all wickedness, and all guile, and hypocrisies, and envies, and all evil speakings, as newborn
babes, long for the spiritual milk." Thus, positively, the
growth can be secured only as the soul receives spiritual
food. The words, "spiritual milk" are often translated

"milk of the word"; and quite possibly the writer has in mind "the word of good tidings" to which he has previously referred as the means of the new birth. Surely the same means must be employed in nourishing the new life; and the main reason for the arrested development of modern Christians is found in their neglect of spiritual food, whereby, as Peter declares, we "may grow . . . unto salvation," that is, unto that full moral maturity, that complete deliverance from sin, which will be realized at the coming of Christ. A longing for such food is the sure proof that we have been "born anew," for if we "have tasted that the Lord is gracious," these first experiences of the loveliness and goodness of Christ will make us yearn to drink more deeply of his exhaustless grace.

Peter next refers to believers as forming a temple, although he unites this figure with that of a priesthood. As "living stones," they are united to Christ, the great Corner Stone who had been set at nought by men but afforded supreme honor by God; cemented to him by faith, and to their fellow Christians by love, they are being built into a glorious house for the indwelling of God, by his Spirit. As a priesthood, they are to offer sacrifices of praise and prayer, of kindness and holiness and love, which will be acceptable to God because presented in the name of Jesus Christ.

Of this spiritual temple the prophets had spoken; they had declared that Christ, as the Corner Stone, was chosen by God, and held in highest honor, and that those who trusted in him should not, as Peter suggests, "be put to shame." The honor, the "preciousness," belonged to believers, but for those who refused to believe on Christ there was only condemnation and loss. The exalted Christ is the touchstone of character; those who spurn his gospel of grace declare their own judgment: "The stone which the builders rejected, the same was made the head of the corner; and, a stone of stumbling, and a rock of offence."

In contrast with the fate of unbelieving Israel, Peter

depicts the privileges of the church, the true people of God: "But ye are an elect race," "chosen," as was the Hebrew people, and a "race," because possessing a common life resulting from the new birth; "a royal priesthood," "royal" as appointed by their King, royal as called to share his dignity and his glory, and "priests," as offering spiritual sacrifices and interceding for men; "a holy nation," a nation separated from others, consecrated unto God, and expected to manifest the moral nature and purity of God; "a people for God's own possession," that is, a people "acquired and possessed by him as a special and peculiar treasure." Such boundless privileges imply great responsibilities: Christians are expected to show forth by life and word, "the excellencies," the virtues, the goodness, the wisdom "of him who called" them, by his Spirit and providence, "out of darkness," the ignorance and night of moral ignorance and unbelief, "into his marvelous light" as revealed in his Son; in time past, whatever their nationality, they really "were no people, but now are the people of God"; they "had not obtained mercy, but now have obtained mercy." Thus the words spoken by Hosea of repentant Israel find their fulfillment in the redeemed, sanctified, beloved followers of Christ.

IV

EXHORTATIONS IN VIEW
OF SPECIAL RELATIONS

Chs. 2:11 to 4:11

a. Sojourners Ch. 2:11-12

> 11 Beloved, I beseech you as sojourners and pilgrims, to
> abstain from fleshly lusts, which war against the soul; 12
> having your behavior seemly among the Gentiles; that,
> wherein they speak against you as evil-doers, they may by
> your good works, which they behold, glorify God in the
> day of visitation.

Here Peter begins a distinct division of his epistle. The
first division consisted in a series of exhortations based
upon the pecular privileges described in his "salutation"
and "thanksgiving," and summarized in the one great word
"salvation." The present series of exhortations enjoins
upon his readers conduct becoming Christians in their
various relations to the state, to the family, and particularly to the heathen society in the midst of which they were
dwelling. The first of these exhortations is wide in its
scope and refers to their whole course of life. In it they
are addressed as "sojourners and pilgrims." Neither of
these words emphasizes the idea which we commonly asso-
ciate with "pilgrims," namely, those who are journeying to
a heavenly land, yet both emphasize a closely related truth.
The first describes those who are in a foreign country, as
"aliens"; the other, those who are remaining in such a country for only a short time; thus both words remind us that
"our citizenship is in heaven," and our stay here is but
brief. Accordingly we are urged to "abstain from fleshly
lusts, which war against the soul"; that is, we are not to

adopt the evil customs of the people among whom we live
or to endanger our spirits the life of which is not brief but
immortal. The "lusts" of which we are warned do not
refer merely to impure, bodily appetites, but to all wrong
and selfish desires and impulses which threaten to take
captive and to destroy the soul.

The special motive given for honorable and consistent
conduct is the effect it might have upon the unbelievers
among whom the readers were sojourning. Christians
were being slandered as irreligious because not worshiping
the heathen gods, as morose and ascetic because refraining
from popular vices, as disloyal to the government because
claiming allegiance to a heavenly King. Peter urges them
to disprove such reports by their pure and noble lives, and
so to conduct themselves that their very accusers might
be won to the faith, and might thank God, in the day of
Christ's appearing, for the good deeds and saving influence
of the Christian pilgrims who had sojourned among them.

b. Citizens   Ch. 2:13-17

> 13 Be subject to every ordinance of man for the Lord's
> sake: whether to the king, as supreme; 14 or unto gov-
> ernors, as sent by him for vengeance on evil-doers and for
> praise to them that do well. 15 For so is the will of God,
> that by well-doing ye should put to silence the ignorance of
> foolish men: 16 as free, and not using your freedom for a
> cloak of wickedness, but as bondservants of God. 17
> Honor all men. Love the brotherhood. Fear God. Honor
> the king.

While Christians are to regard themselves as citizens
of heaven, yet they are to remember that, in a very real
sense, they are now citizens upon earth; they are subject
to human government, and are to show their fidelity to
Christ by their loyalty to the state. Heavenly privileges
and prospects are to make them not less faithful but rather
more faithful to present obligations and duties. Thus,
having addressed his readers as "pilgrims" and having

given them a general exhortation to right conduct, Peter's first specific command relates to the duties of Christian citizens. They are urged to obey all the requirements and demands of civil rulers, and to do so as thereby pleasing and serving Christ: "Be subject to every ordinance of man for the Lord's sake." These Christians were to obey "the king," by which was meant the emperor, probably Nero, and likewise his representatives, the "governors," whose tasks consisted largely in punishing "evil-doers" and in protecting and rewarding those who did well. Peter declares such loyalty, even to such imperial monsters, to be the will of God, and the best way in which to silence the slanders which were current in reference to Christians. Of course, in a very true sense, followers of Christ are "free"; they are responsible to their Lord; they are not to obey the emperor if he asks them to act contrary to the will of their Lord; they also, at times, may be asked to judge whether a government is lawful and worthy of support; liberty, however, is not license; it is no excuse for disloyalty, sedition, or treason; Christians are not to use the word "freedom" as "a cloak of wickedness"; even an imperfect government is better than anarchy; freedom is deserved and can rightly be enjoyed only by those who are "bondservants of God." Such men will "honor all men." By this phrase Peter seems to indicate the observance of the proprieties of life in showing the respect demanded by custom to persons of various rank and position; yet the command includes a proper consideration of the sacred rights of all men, even the most weak and humble and obscure.

"Love the brotherhood." While all men must be treated with respect, we should show a peculiar affection and regard for those who are one with us in Christ. "Fear God. Honor the king." A reverential awe is to be felt toward God; this is not inconsistent with devoted loyalty to the king; in fact the purport of the whole paragraph shows that the most faithful servant of God will surely be the most patriotic supporter of the state.

c. Servants   Ch. 2:18-25

18 Servants, be in subjection to your masters with all fear; not only to the good and gentle, but also to the froward. 19 For this is acceptable, if for conscience toward God a man endureth griefs, suffering wrongfully. 20 For what glory is it, if, when ye sin, and are buffeted for it, ye shall take it patiently? but if, when ye do well, and suffer for it, ye shall take it patiently, this is acceptable with God. 21 For hereunto were ye called: because Christ also suffered for you, leaving you an example, that ye should follow his steps: 22 who did no sin, neither was guile found in his mouth: 23 who, when he was reviled, reviled not again; when he suffered, threatened not; but committed himself to him that judgeth righteously: 24 who his own self bare our sins in his body upon the tree, that we, having died unto sins, might live unto righteousness; by whose stripes ye were healed. 25 For ye were going astray like sheep; but are now returned unto the Shepherd and Bishop of your souls.

In urging upon his readers conduct becoming to Christians in the various relations of life, Peter first emphasizes the duties of citizens to the state; he next dwells upon the relation of servants to their masters. He does not address them as slaves, the word employed by Paul, but as "household servants," a term which, in that day, included free men and women, even clerks and musicians and teachers and physicians; thus the passage applies to the attitude of all employees toward their employers and bears upon the vexed modern problems of labor and capital.

The one comprehensive exhortation is to submission: "Servants, be in subjection to your masters with all fear." This "subjection" however, is like that previously suggested toward kings and governors: it implies not only obedience but also loyalty; servants are not only to submit but to be faithful and to advance the interests of their masters. The "fear" is not of punishment, but denotes anxious fidelity and deference under all circumstances, the

desire to avoid all offense.   As submission to a cruel
tyrant like Nero was a special test of loyalty to the state,
so the proof of faithfulness in servants was found in their
obedience not only to masters who were kind and considerate, but also to the "froward," the unreasonable, the
cruel, and the unjust   It would be specially acceptable to
God, if for his sake, because of obligation to him and
strengthened by the thought of his presence, they would
endure patiently sufferings which were undeserved, blows
and scourgings even when they had merited praise.

Peter makes no reference here to "masters" and their
reciprocal duties, not so much because the larger number
of his readers were servants as because he is dwelling in
this section of his epistle upon the Christian graces of submission and meekness.   Of course masters are required
to be gentle and just.   The patient fidelity of their servants only increases their own obligation to be reasonable,
fair, and generous.   Nor does this paragraph forbid employees to use all lawful means to secure their rights and
to advance their interests.   Here the exhortation is to patience under wrongs for which there is no remedy.   Endurance of undeserved punishment, when there can be no
redress, is here declared to be a ground of glorying and of
praise.

Christians are encouraged to such patient endurance
by the example of their Lord.   When they were summoned
to follow him, such sufferings were involved in their call;
they should expect them to be part of their experience.
They should follow in his footsteps "who did no sin," and
yet suffered a cruel death.   Peter specially calls to mind
the uncomplaining meekness of Christ at the time of his
trial and crucifixion, and declares that he was suffering
innocently, but for our sakes: "Who his own self bare our
sins in his body upon the tree."   The language is descrip-
tive of sacrifice; the death on the cross was atoning; Christ
took upon him the dread consequences of our guilt; the
emphasis, however, is laid upon the purpose of his death,

which was not only that we might break with sin, once and for all, but very definitely that we "might live unto righteousness." "By whose stripes ye were healed." The marks of the cruel scourge upon his quivering flesh were but signs of that suffering which for our sakes he endured, when submitting to the death of a slave. Surely servants, for his sake, should endure patiently the severest wrongs. To him they owed their salvation; like lost sheep they were wandering farther and farther from virtue and from God, but now they have been brought to find in Christ the Shepherd and the Guardian of their souls.

d. Wives and Husbands Ch. 3:1-7

1 *In like manner, ye wives,* be *in subjection to your own husbands; that, even if any obey not the word, they may without the word be gained by the behavior of their wives; 2 beholding your chaste behavior* coupled *with fear. 3 Whose* adorning *let it not be the outward adorning of braiding the hair, and of wearing jewels of gold, or of putting on apparel; 4 but* let it be *the hidden man of the heart, in the incorruptible* apparel *of a meek and quiet spirit, which is in the sight of God of great price. 5 For after this manner aforetime the holy women also, who hoped in God, adorned themselves, being in subjection to their own husbands: 6 as Sarah obeyed Abraham, calling him lord: whose children ye now are, if ye do well, and are not put in fear by any terror.*

7 *Ye husbands, in like manner, dwell with* your *wives according to knowledge, giving honor unto the woman, as unto the weaker vessel, as being also joint-heirs of the grace of life; to the end that your prayers be not hindered.*

As citizens were to be loyal to the state even under the reign of a Caesar, as servants were to obey masters who were cruel and unjust, so wives were to render loving obedience to their husbands even when the latter were not Christians: "In like manner, ye wives, be in subjection to your own husbands." The exhortation is not popular at the present day; many are arguing that as despotism is not to be tolerated in government, nor slavery in society, so obedience to husbands is no longer necessary in the family. Of course no wife need feel compelled to act contrary to conscience or duty; of course no personal inferiority is implied; of course there are sacred rights which none should dare invade; yet upon Christian wives there ever rests the obligation of patient submission to their husbands. The special reason here assigned is the possibility that unbelieving husbands might be won for Christ by "the behavior of their wives." Even though they had rejected the gospel they might "be gained" without preaching, as they read sermons without words, written in the eloquent language of pure conduct and respectful demeanor, of "chaste behavior coupled with fear."

In married life, admiration and affection can be retained not so much by extravagant adornment of the body as by the irresistible charm of spirit and disposition: "Whose adorning let it not be the outward adorning of braiding the hair, and of wearing jewels of gold, or of putting on apparel; but let it be the hidden man of the heart, in the incorruptible apparel of a meek and quiet spirit." This is no prohibition of jewelry or becoming costumes; it is a comparison between two forms of attractiveness. The apparel which wears best and is never out of style is the "meek and quiet spirit" which never worries or causes worry; it is pleasing not only to men but also to God.

As a model for Christian matrons, Peter cites the godly women of old whose chief charm consisted in their loyal devotion, who "adorned themselves, being in subjection to their own husbands"; in particular, he mentions Sarah, whose attitude of respect and reverence was illustrated by a single term of address, she "obeyed Abraham, calling him lord." All who are like her in spirit are, in this sense, her "children," just as all believers are children of Abraham, the "father of the faithful." Obedience and submission, however, do not mean anxious fear, or continual dread, or cowering terror; these are not attractive to men or pleasing to God; the wife is to be sure that her conduct is right and shaped with due regard to her husband, but she is not to be "put in fear by any terror."

Husbands, on the other hand, are not to presume upon their position or to forget their mutual obligations. "Obedience" on the part of a wife will involve nothing of humiliation or distress if a husband is conducting himself as a Christian. While he recognizes in his wife certain natural limitations of strength, he will not regard this as an excuse for tyranny or injustice, but with true chivalry will find it an occasion for more tenderness and sympathy and reverence, "giving honor unto the woman, as unto the weaker vessel." Least of all will the submission of a wife imperil her happiness and highest good, when the husband remembers their absolute spiritual equality as joint heirs of the life eternal granted them by the grace of God. One who realizes this grace will be humble in spirit; he cannot be inconsiderate or unkind; he will seek to show devoted love, to maintain that perfect human harmony and concord without which fellowship with God is impossible. The first and last words of the paragraph form a significant and striking rule for husbands: "Dwell with your wives . . . that your prayers be not hindered."

e. Innocent Sufferers   Ch. 3:8-22

8 Finally, be ye all likeminded, compassionate, loving as brethren, tenderhearted, humbleminded: 9 not rendering evil for evil, or reviling for reviling; but contrariwise blessing; for hereunto were ye called, that ye should inherit a blessing.
10 For,
He that would love life,
And see good days,
Let him refrain his tongue from evil,
And his lips that they speak no guile:
11 And let him turn away from evil, and do good;
Let him seek peace, and pursue it.
12 For the eyes of the Lord are upon the righteous,

And his ears unto their supplication:
But the face of the Lord is upon them that do evil.

13 And who is he that will harm you, if ye be zealous of
that which is good? 14 But even if ye should suffer for
righteousness' sake, blessed are ye: and fear not their fear,
neither be troubled; 15 but sanctify in your hearts Christ
as Lord: being ready always to give answer to every man
that asketh you a reason concerning the hope that is in
you, yet with meekness and fear: 16 having a good conscience; that, wherein ye are spoken against, they may be
put to shame who revile your good manner of life in Christ.
17 For it is better, if the will of God should so will, that
ye suffer for well-doing than for evil-doing. 18 Because
Christ also suffered for sins once, the righteous for the unrighteous, that he might bring us to God; being put to death
in the flesh, but made alive in the spirit; 19 in which also
he went and preached unto the spirits in prison, 20 that
aforetime were disobedient, when the longsuffering of God
waited in the days of Noah, while the ark was a preparing,
wherein few, that is, eight souls, were saved through water:
21 which also after a true likeness doth now save you, even
baptism, not the putting away of the filth of the flesh, but
the interrogation of a good conscience toward God, through
the resurrection of Jesus Christ; 22 who is on the right
hand of God, having gone into heaven; angels and authorities and powers being made subject unto him.

Having given special instructions to citizens and servants and wives, Peter speaks more broadly to all his
readers as to their consistent conduct as Christians. In
these more general exhortations the keynote is still the
same; Peter continues to emphasize the duty of submission, and to suggest that while there are other graces, and
while life has much of happiness and blessing, still the followers of Christ will be like him in encountering many
sufferings. But by faith in him they can endure patiently
and will see that the final issue of their sufferings is enlarged usefulness and blessedness.

"Finally," writes the apostle, as if his words were reach-

ing a climax, and as if he would turn from special classes
to address all Christians, "be ye all likeminded," one in
sentiment, of "one accord"; "compassionate," sympathizing with the sorrows and also with the blessings of others;
"loving as brethren," that is, as belonging to the one family
of Christian believers; "tenderhearted," "humbleminded";
"not rendering evil for evil, or reviling for reviling; but
contrariwise blessing; for hereunto were ye called, that ye
should inherit a blessing."   Earlier in his letter Peter has
suggested that we are "called" to unmerited sufferings; he
is to emphasize that truth later in this paragraph; but he
first reminds us that the issue will be blessing, and that we
are as truly heirs of happiness as heirs of trial.   Peter further reminds us that life is not all hardship, that one who
is kind and humble and loving will usually have good days
and will be able to secure peace, especially when he trusts
God, who is a righteous God, neither unconscious of the
needs of his people nor indifferent to the sins of those that
do evil.   This truth Peter enforces by a quotation from the
Thirty-fourth Psalm, which is in itself a hymn of comfort
for those who suffer innocently.   Peter suggests that, usually, those who are ardent lovers of good will not be mo-
lested; no one will wish to injure them: "And who is he
that will harm you, if ye be zealous of that which is good?"

Nevertheless, Christians need not be surprised at persecution; it may come, even to the most upright.   When
it comes it is to be regarded as a possible channel of blessing: "But even if ye should suffer for righteousness' sake,
blessed are ye: and fear not their fear," do not be terrified
by the threats of such enemies, "neither be troubled"; let
the one object of your reverential fear, of your trust, of
your love, be Christ: "Sanctify in your hearts Christ as
Lord."   As to your enemies, be ready to meet them with
intelligent replies; they may ridicule your beliefs and particularly your expectations of heavenly glory, but be "ready
always to give answer to every man that asketh you a reason concerning the hope that is in you, yet with meekness

and fear." Pride and conceit will weaken your defense of the Christian faith; spiritual realities are not capable of mathematical proof; you may be confident of your positions, yet you are not to answer your opponents with bitterness and pride. The best possible reply to those who criticize your beliefs and malign your character will be given by a life of purity and sincerity and charity: "having a good conscience: that, wherein ye are spoken against, they may be put to shame who revile your good manner of life in Christ." If persecution is allowed to come, it is better that it shall have no ground or justification in your unkind words or inconsistent deeds.

Persecution and distress, however, cannot permanently injure or impair the helpful influence of innocent sufferers. The example of Christ is full of comfort and inspiration. His sufferings, even his death, only enlarged the sphere of his activity: for while his body was in the tomb, he went and preached to the spirits in the underworld, and after his resurrection he ascended into heaven and was given the place of supreme power. Surely his sufferings were undeserved: he "suffered for sins once, the righteous for the unrighteous"; the purpose was "that he might bring us to God"; this great end was achieved, and we now have access through him to God. It could be achieved only by his death; but even while he continued under the power of death he went to the place of disembodied spirits, or, to use the words of the Apostles' Creed, "he descended into hell," by which is meant, to a "place of detention," of waiting for final judgment; he preached to "the spirits in prison," that had rejected the message of Noah in the days when the ark was being built. In the ark only eight souls escaped, saved by the very water which destroyed the impenitent and which purified the ancient world. So we believers are saved by the water of baptism, if by baptism we mean not a mere external rite but a spiritual cleansing which ends the old life of sin and begins a new life of holiness. Such salvation is communicated to us by the faith which is confessed at the time of baptism; it has been made possible through the resurrection of Christ, who gives new life to believers. Thus the unmerited sufferings of Christ resulted not only in his preaching to the imprisoned dead, but, as he rose from the dead, in giving eternal life to all who trust him; the further result is again voiced by the Creed: "He ascended into heaven, and sitteth on the right hand of God the Father Almighty."

This whole passage which speaks of preaching to "the spirits in prison" is full of difficulty and mystery. Many interpretations have been attempted; they differ as to the time and place and substance and results of this preaching. A popular view is that which suggests that the preaching was done by Christ, in the person of the Holy Spirit, in the actual days of Noah, and not between the death and the resurrection of Christ as the words more naturally suggest. There is less danger of an incorrect exposition of the words than in the inferences based on the various interpretations. These words do not prove the existence of purgatory, or countenance the abuses connected with the belief in purgatorial sufferings. Nor do they support the theory of a "second chance" for all who die in impenitence. Nor yet do they give ground for believing that all men will be saved whatever their earthly lives have been. The teachings about purgatory, and "second probation," and universal salvation, are not sanctioned by Scripture; these are mere unwarranted inferences from statements which are full of mystery. Here it is not safe to go beyond what is written. The reference to "the spirits in prison" is but a parenthesis, an illustration, The main teaching of the passage is perfectly simple and plain. The purpose of the writer was not to awaken vague speculations, but to give practical encouragement. He assures us that innocent sufferers can sustain no abiding loss; if they are united with Christ, even death will be but gain. Their spirits will continue to live, they "depart" to "be with Christ"; "absent from the body" is to be "at home with the

Lord." Some day the dead will share his resurrection victory, and will enjoy in all its fullness his heavenly glory.

f. *Opposed by Sinners   Ch. 4:1-6*

1 Forasmuch then as Christ suffered in the flesh, arm ye yourselves also with the same mind; for he that hath suffered in the flesh hath ceased from sin; 2 that ye no longer should live the rest of your time in the flesh to the lusts of men, but to the will of God. 3 For the time past may suffice to have wrought the desire of the Gentiles, and to have walked in lasciviousness, lusts, winebibbings, revellings, carousings, and abominable idolatries: 4 wherein they think it strange that ye run not with them into the same excess of riot, speaking evil of you: 5 who shall give account to him that is ready to judge the living and the dead. 6 For unto this end was the gospel preached even to the dead, that they might be judged indeed according to men in the flesh, but live according to God in the spirit.

The subject of this paragraph is not new. Peter is still considering the unmerited sufferings to which his readers are compelled to submit; but here he emphasizes the evil character of their enemies and encourages his readers to fight against their former evil habits and the prevalent pagan vices. The memory of the sufferings of Christ and their blessed issue, of which Peter had just written, should strengthen believers for the conflict: "Forasmuch then as Christ suffered in the flesh, arm ye yourselves also with the same mind." As Christ suffered from the opposition of an evil world, his followers should be prepared for the same experience, especially by the thought of the results of such suffering. These would be, in the case of Christians, moral purity and a definite break with sin; "for he that hath suffered in the flesh hath ceased from sin." It is a general law of spiritual life that suffering purifies; there are exceptions to the rule: sometimes it hardens and embitters; but where it is endured for the sake of Christ and with the memories of what he endured and thereby achieved, it re-

sults in a perfecting of character. Of this general law,
Peter here makes a special application. One whose sufferings have been caused by his opposition to sin, by his un-
willingness to imitate sinners, has surely, in so far, "ceased
from sin." He is not free from the assaults of sin, but the
consciousness of his experience, and the thought of Christ,
will enable him to regard his very sufferings as badges of
his fidelity, as proofs of his loyalty to his Master. He will
be reminded that the lines have been definitely drawn and
that he now belongs to those who for the rest of their lives
are not to be directed by the "lusts of men," but by "the
will of God."

We may be encouraged further to "arm" ourselves
against our sufferings and our temptations, when we remember how large a portion of our time has already been
spent in unholy living; as Peter says with solemn irony, it
"may suffice," or "it is quite enough." Not all of his
readers may have been guilty of the impurity and intem-
perance and idolatry of which he speaks; yet even Jews
did fall into these pagan practices and excesses; but whatever the conduct had been before accepting Christ, the
time remaining was all too brief for the service of the
Master.

Such a new life of holiness is sure to be the occasion of
opposition, of misinterpretation, and of abuse; but the
final judge is God; to him these sinful slanderers "shall
give account"; by him those who are being persecuted for
righteousness' sake will be vindicated; from his judgment
none can escape. It will extend to the dead as well as
to the living. For this reason, that the judgment might
be absolutely just, "was the gospel preached even to the
dead, that they might be judged indeed according to men
in the flesh," according to their works when on earth,
and as already suffering the penalty of physical death, but
might "live according to God in the spirit," that is, might
be pardoned and become heirs of eternal life. The reference here seems to be to the previous mysterious passage
which spoke of the preaching to "the spirits in prison."

Both statements are obscure; the practical bearing is plain. Here the simple truth is emphasized that all men, without exception, are to be judged by God, a truth intended to encourage those who are seeking to keep from sin, and to warn those by whom they are opposed.

g. Expecting the Coming of Christ   Ch. 4:7-11

7 But the end of all things is at hand: be ye therefore of sound mind, and be sober unto prayer: 8 above all things being fervent in your love among yourselves; for love covereth a multitude of sins: 9 using hospitality one to another without murmuring: 10 according as each hath received a gift, ministering it among yourselves, as good stewards of the manifold grace of God; 11 if any man speaketh, speaking as it were oracles of God; if any man ministereth, ministering as of the strength which God supplieth: that in all things God may be glorified through Jesus Christ, whose is the glory and the dominion for ever and ever. Amen.

The return of our Lord has always furnished the supreme motive for consistent Christian living. Thus when Peter has given special exhortations to right conduct as citizens, servants, wives, and innocent sufferers, he closes this section of his epistle with a series of general exhortations based on the hope of the coming of Christ: "But the end of all things is at hand: be ye therefore of sound mind, and be sober unto prayer." To be "of sound mind" denotes "self-control"; this quality together with clearness and sobriety of mind, are urged in order that prayer may not be interrupted. It should be noted that a very different state of mind is too frequently associated with the expectation of the return of Christ. Fear, idle curiosity, restless excitement, neglect of duty, too commonly attend popular teaching concerning the Second Advent. This has been caused by false statements relative to the time of the Advent and by neglecting the consideration of events which are predicted as preceding the return of Christ. How soon these predictions may be fulfilled no one can tell. They may occur in any generation. Their consummation, in the appearing of Christ, is the supreme hope of the church; but the expectation should inspire us to a faithful performance of duty in the state, in society, in the family, and in the church. Christians should be self-controlled, sober, and prayerful.

Further, they should be "fervent in . . . love" among themselves—this in view of the return of Christ—and such love should be "persevering" because it covers "a multitude of sins," which probably means that it covers the sins of others, is generous and forgiving.

Two special manifestations of love are now mentioned: first, "hospitality," and second, the use of talents. In the early church the grace of "hospitality" was much emphasized; it did not denote the entertainment of friends but the relief of travelers; as inns were rare and poor, as the extension of the church depended upon the work of itinerant evangelists, the need of receiving strangers into their homes was apparent to all Christians; yet it did require love, it did offer occasions for imposition, for resentment, and for murmuring.

Secondly, love was demanded in the use of special talents; these were to be regarded as trusts committed to Christians as stewards, to be used for the benefit of others and for which they were to render an account to their Lord. Thus if a man exercised the gift of public speech, he should do so not in such a way as to win praise for himself, but so as to help others, and he should speak as one who was uttering messages which were not his own but which had been given him by God. So, too, in caring for the poor, or sick, or needy, one should show no pride or patronage, but should humbly acknowledge that his ability for doing good had been entrusted to him by God. Thus Christians were in all things to seek not their own glory but the glory of God through Jesus Christ, to whom should be ascribed the glory and the dominion forever and ever.

V

EXHORTATIONS IN VIEW OF SPECIAL TRIALS

Chs. 4:12 to 5:11

a. Exhortation to Steadfastness in Suffering   Ch. 4:12-19

12 Beloved, think it not strange concerning the fiery trial among you, which cometh upon you to prove you, as though a strange thing happened unto you: 13 but insomuch as ye are partakers of Christ's sufferings, rejoice; that at the revelation of his glory also ye may rejoice with exceeding joy. 14 If ye are reproached for the name of Christ, blessed are ye; because the Spirit of glory and the Spirit of God resteth upon you. 15 For let none of you suffer as a murderer, or a thief, or an evil-doer, or as a meddler in other men's matters: 16 but if a man suffer as a Christian, let him not be ashamed; but let him glorify God in this name. 17 For the time is come for judgment to begin at the house of God: and if it begin first at us, what shall be the end of them that obey not the gospel of God? 18 And if the righteous is scarcely saved, where shall the ungodly and sinner appear? 19 Wherefore let them also that suffer according to the will of God commit their souls in well-doing unto a faithful Creator.

Here Peter begins the third series of the exhortations which compose the epistle. The first were in view of the special privileges his readers were enjoying, the second in view of their special relations in the state and in society; these are given in view of the sufferings they are called to endure. All in the series are closely united, and particularly by the mention of sufferings made in each of the two preceding divisions and only further emphasized in this last. In every case, too, the great incentive to steadfast endurance is found in the hope of the return of Christ, and in the deliverance and glory which he will bring.

The sufferings are here described as a "fiery trial," an ordeal, a trial by fire: "Beloved, think it not strange concerning the fiery trial among you." Christians should expect persecution and suffering; they should not be surprised by trials or regard them as something foreign to their lot; these trials were testing their faith and purifying their characters. If the Master was made to endure sufferings, it should not be regarded as strange that his servants were compelled to endure the same; they should rejoice because, as they trusted him and were persecuted for his sake, they were really "partakers of Christ's sufferings." Such courage should be shown in order that when Christ appeared they might enjoy a truer rapture and exaltation: "that at the revelation of his glory also ye may rejoice with exceeding joy." Fellowship in the sufferings of Christ is to be regarded confidently as an assurance of partnership in his glory. "If ye are reproached for the name of Christ, blessed are ye; because the Spirit of glory and the Spirit of God resteth upon you"; if, that is, you suffer for bearing the name of Christ, and for a life consistent with such a profession; for such a life is possible only by the power of his divine Spirit, and as this is also the "Spirit of glory," his present manifestation is an assurance of the perfected glory you will enjoy at the appearing of Christ. On the other hand one must be certain that his sufferings are not deserved: "For let none of you suffer as a murderer, or a thief, or an evil-doer, or as a meddler in other men's matters." The last phrase is a peculiar one and may possibly mean "one who busies himself about matters not befitting a Christian." "But if a man suffer as a Christian, let him not be ashamed; but let him glorify God in this name."

A second reason for steadfastness is found in the fact that these sufferings are to be viewed as an actual beginning of the judgment coming upon the world at the return of Christ; the "fiery trial" was a herald of coming deliverance. Such the mold of prophecy has ever been; and as our Lord predicted, in the midst of a "great tribulation," which develops out of these age-long trials and sufferings, when there is "distress of nations," when "the powers of the heavens shall be shaken, . . . then shall they see the Son of man coming in a cloud with power and great glory. But when these things begin to come to pass, look up, and lift up your heads; because your redemption draweth nigh." This seems to be the meaning of Peter in saying "For the time is come for judgment to begin at the house of God," for the people of his household, for the very readers of this letter, sufferings have already begun. However, if Christians now suffer, what then will be the fate of unbelievers; and "if the righteous," the follower of Christ, "is scarcely saved," that is, only after enduring such sufferings and tribulation, "where shall the ungodly and sinner appear," what will be their doom? Therefore, in view of the sure deliverance which is coming "let them also that suffer according to the will of God commit their souls in well-doing unto a faithful Creator." Let us submit to his will and seek to do his will, trusting that through all the mystery of suffering he cares for his own.

b. Exhortation to Fidelity   Ch. 5:1-4

1 The elders therefore among you I exhort, who am a fellow-elder, and a witness of the sufferings of Christ, who am also a partaker of the glory that shall be revealed: 2 Tend the flock of God which is among you, exercising the oversight, not of constraint, but willingly, according to the will of God; nor yet for filthy lucre, but of a ready mind; 3 neither as lording it over the charge allotted to you, but making yourselves ensamples to the flock. 4 And when the chief Shepherd shall be manifested, ye shall receive the crown of glory that fadeth not away.

In times of trial, the task of religious teachers is one of peculiar responsibility; a congregation in distress has special need of pastoral care. Thus, when Peter has urged his readers to steadfastness in suffering, he now turns to the officers of the church to urge upon them faithfulness in the discharge of their duties. These officers are called "elders," a name given at first to all who exercised rule and authority among the Christians; it is identical with the word "bishop" as in the next verse these officers are described as "exercising the oversight" or, literally, "doing the work of bishops"; the word "elder" suggests the mature age which qualified one for the office; the word "bishop" indicates the duties of the office as being those of spiritual oversight; another identical term is "presbyter," and the band of elders formed the "presbytery," or church court. Peter here describes himself as "a fellow-elder," to appeal to their affection; but to indicate his authority he declares that from personal observation he is one who bears testimony to the sufferings of Christ and who is to be "a partaker of the glory that shall be revealed" when Christ returns.

In his exhortation, Peter indicates another title of these "elders" or "bishops," namely, "pastors": "Tend the flock of God which is among you," fill the office of spiritual shepherds, not as a mere matter of necessary, professional duty, but with a willing mind, as serving God, not like hirelings for the mere earning of the salary you are paid, but gladly and eagerly, not acting as lords and tyrants in the congregation entrusted to you, but making yourselves examples for the flock; your earthly recompense may be small, but when Christ, "the chief Shepherd" shall appear, then you "shall receive the crown of glory that fadeth not away."

c. Exhortations to Humility, Trust, Vigilance, and Constancy   Ch. 5:5-11

5 Likewise, ye younger, be subject unto the elder. Yea, all of you gird yourselves with humility, to serve one another: for God resisteth the proud, but giveth grace to the humble. 6 Humble yourselves therefore under the mighty

*hand of God, that he may exalt you in due time; 7 casting
all your anxiety upon him, because he careth for you. 8
Be sober, be watchful: your adversary the devil, as a roaring lion, walketh about, seeking whom he may devour: 9
whom withstand stedfast in your faith, knowing that the
same sufferings are accomplished in your brethren who are
in the world. 10 And the God of all grace, who called you
unto his eternal glory in Christ, after that ye have suffered
a little while, shall himself perfect, establish, strengthen
you. 11 To him be the dominion for ever and ever.*

Amen.

The word "elder" may denote either a church officer or
a man advanced in years. In the last paragraph it meant
the former, here it possibly means the latter. Younger
persons are urged to render respectful obedience to church
officers, or to Christians who possess the maturity and
wisdom of age. In fact, all Christians are urged to "gird
themselves" with "humility," probably as with the "garb
of slaves," to be ready to render to one another every possible service, as the garment of humility is always an essential equipment for wide helpfulness. Especially toward
God is humility to be shown: "Humble yourselves . . .
under the mighty hand of God, that he may exalt you in
due time"; it is in his mysterious providence that afflictions
come, but his power also brings deliverance in his appointed time. We are to look to him in humble trust, casting the whole burden of our anxiety upon him, believing
that he lovingly cares for us.

"Casting all . . . anxiety upon him" does not relieve
us, however, from the responsibility of being watchful
against temptation. The Christian must be "sober" and
"watchful" because his "adversary the devil, as a roaring
lion, walketh about, seeking whom he may devour." This
graphic figure of speech may indicate some of the peculiar
temptations of the readers, the opposition of their ad-
versaries, the false charges of their slanderers; but it also
symbolizes the cruelty and the craft, the restless activity

and terrifying threats, which ever characterize the foul tempter, the enemy of our souls. We are encouraged on two grounds to oppose this enemy, with steadfast loyalty to Christ, with unshaken constancy of faith: first, because our trials and temptations are common to the whole brotherhood of Christians, they are not peculiar to us, they are being courageously endured and resisted by countless others; and secondly, because God, the Author of all grace, who called us "unto his eternal glory in Christ," after the comparatively brief time of our distress, will himself make us perfect through our sufferings, will make us so firm in the faith that we shall be shaken by no alarms, will give us such spiritual strength that we shall never be overcome; all power is his, he will supply our every need: "To him be the dominion for ever and ever. Amen."

VI
THE CONCLUSION
Ch. 5:12-14

a. The Bearer and Purpose of the Letter   Ch. 5:12

12 By Silvanus, our faithful brother, as I account him,
I have written unto you briefly, exhorting, and testifying
that this is the true grace of God: stand ye fast therein.

In his closing sentences, Peter first mentions Silvanus, to
whom he had dictated the letter, and by whom, possibly, it
was being sent.   He will be remembered by the name of
"Silas" or "Silvanus," as the trusted companion whom Paul
had chosen for his second great missionary journey; he
has won the like confidence of Peter, and is here described
as his "faithful" Christian "brother."

Peter next describes his letter as being very brief in
comparison with all he should like to write, and as con-
taining not only serious exhortations, but also a solemn
attestation that the faith held by his readers is "the true
grace of God"; this grace should be shown in the conduct
he has prescribed; in this faith he urges them to "stand
. . . fast."

b. The Salutation and Benediction   Ch. 5:13-14

13 She that is in Babylon, elect together with you, sa-
luteth you; and so doth Mark my son.   14 Salute one another with a kiss of love.
Peace be unto you all that are in Christ.

In the closing salutation, the phrase "she that is in
Babylon" has been the occasion of endless conjecture and
discussion.   It has been considered by many to be mystical
and symbolical and to mean "the church in Rome," since

Rome was regarded as like Babylon in its opposition to the people and the cause of God. The importance of the theory consists in the fact that it affords the only Scriptural support for the tradition that Peter visited Rome, and wrote this epistle from that imperial city. That "Babylon" is used figuratively is, however, a mere conjecture and never has been proved. With this salutation Peter adds another from Mark, the early companion of Paul and Barnabas, the author of the Second Gospel; he is affectionately called a "son," a spiritual child of Peter, by whom probably he had been brought to Christ.

After urging the members of the church to greet one another with the kiss of charity to signify their brotherly love, Peter closes his epistle with the prayer and benediction: "Peace be unto you all that are in Christ."

THE SECOND EPISTLE OF PETER

THE SECOND EPISTLE
OF PETER

While serious doubt has been felt as to the authorship of this epistle, it is most probable that it should be assigned to the apostle whose name it bears. He was now far advanced in years. Long before, when the risen Lord met his disciples in the morning twilight by the sea, he predicted that Peter, when old, would endure martyrdom for the sake of his Master whom he was bidden to follow not only in service but in suffering. The day of supreme testing was at hand, as he penned this epistle. "The putting off of my tabernacle cometh swiftly," he writes, "even as our Lord Jesus Christ signified unto me." However he sounds no note of despondency, fear, or gloom; his message, like that of his First Epistle, is radiant with hope. His thought is centered upon the coming of Christ; he still rejoices to think of the time "when the chief Shepherd shall be manifested" from whom he would receive "the crown of glory that fadeth not away." Something of the splendor of that crowning day he now declares was witnessed by him on the holy mount, when he saw the transfigured Christ; long years have passed, but the vivid memory of that "Majestic Glory" is set forth as a ground of his present, triumphant faith. The writer further declares of himself that he has written a previous epistle of a somewhat similar character; that he is on intimate terms with Paul, whom he calls "our beloved brother," and with whose letters he declares himself familiar. Surely it is idle to conjecture who this writer may have been if he was not Peter the apostle, whom its references so definitely depict.

The readers, then, would be the same as those of the

previous epistle, the Christian converts scattered throughout various provinces of what is now known as Asia Minor. Their condition, however, is now different, or their circumstances are somewhat altered. The particular perils by which they are threatened are not from without but from within the churches. Their dangers are not from the persecutions of Jews and pagans, but from the pernicious influences of professed Christians, "false teachers" who have appeared, who are increasing in number, who deny the Lord not only by their doctrines but by their impure and unholy lives. The truth which they attack particularly is that of the return of Christ, and their conduct corresponds with their unbelief; because of his long delay they mock at "the promise of his coming," "walking after their own lusts."

To warn against such errors in teaching and to exhort to holiness in living, his epistle was written. Its supreme word is "knowledge." As the source is in God, as the chief object is Christ, as it is associated with "grace," this "knowledge" is not merely a mental but also a spiritual attainment. It can be increased by the practice of Christian virtues, and the readers are urged to "grow in the grace and knowledge of our Lord and Saviour Jesus Christ." The special truth, however, with which this "knowledge" is here concerned is that which the false teachers deny, namely, the return of Christ. This truth is shown to be attested both by the transfiguration glory of Christ and the word of inspired prophecy; the punishment of the false teachers is set forth and their character definitely described; the certainty of the coming of Christ and its attendant judgments are affirmed; and the plea is made for such conduct and character on the part of believers as may be worthy of their faith and hope.

It may be helpful to suggest for the three chapters of this epistle the following outline:

1. The Knowledge of Christ   *II Peter, ch. 1*
    a. The Salutation: The Gift of Knowledge   *Ch. 1:1-4*
    b. The Exhortation: The Growth of Knowledge *Ch. 1:5-11*
    c. The Promise: The Grounds of Knowledge   *Ch. 1:12-21*
2. The Teachers of Error   *Ch. 2*
    a. Their Punishment   *Ch. 2:1-9*
    b. Their Character and Conduct   *Ch. 2:10-16*
    c. Their Evil Influence   *Ch. 2:17-22*
3. The Coming of Christ   *Ch. 3*
    a. The Certainty   *Ch. 3:1-7*
    b. The Time and Circumstances   *Ch. 3:8-13*
    c. The Consequent Exhortation   *Ch. 3:14-18*

I
THE KNOWLEDGE
OF CHRIST
II Peter, ch. 1

a. The Salutation: The Gift of Knowledge   Ch. 1:1-4

1 Simon Peter, a servant and apostle of Jesus Christ, to them that have obtained a like precious faith with us in the righteousness of our God and the Saviour Jesus Christ: 2 Grace to you and peace be multiplied in the knowledge of God and of Jesus our Lord; 3 seeing that his divine power hath granted unto us all things that pertain unto life and godliness, through the knowledge of him that called us by his own glory and virtue; 4 whereby he hath granted unto us his precious and exceeding great promises; that through these ye may become partakers of the divine nature, having escaped from the corruption that is in the world by lust.

It is possible that as Peter calls himself "Simon," he may have had in mind the early days before he met Jesus, when that was his familiar name. It is also possible that, as he calls himself an "apostle," he may have wished to suggest his authority as a man specially commissioned by his Lord, and also, that, as he calls himself "a bondservant . . . of Jesus Christ," he may have wished thus to place himself upon an equality with his readers.   This last purpose was surely accomplished by the beautiful phrase in which these readers are addressed.   Here he not only appeals to their sympathy by a touch of tactful courtesy, but he gives a message to Christians of all times by a stroke of spiritual insight.   He writes "to them that have obtained a like precious faith with us in the righteousness of our God and the Saviour Jesus Christ."   That is, faith gives exactly the

same spiritual privileges to all, whether the most famous
of apostles or the most obscure of believers; this faith is
"obtained by lot" or given by the grace and mercy of God,
without any desert or merit of man; it brings with it equal
privileges because of the absolute justice or "righteousness
of our God and the Saviour Jesus Christ."

The salutation, "Grace to you and peace be multiplied,"
is quite familiar in form, but it is connected with a unique
phrase and one which sounds the keynote of the epistle;
"in the knowledge of God and of Jesus our Lord." This
"knowledge" is the channel of "grace," it is the ground of
"peace," it is the means of salvation, it is the instrument of
all blessings. Peter writes to remind Christians of the
content of this knowledge, to warn them of apostate teachers who are opposing it in the interests of a false "knowledge," to encourage them to value and to develop this true
knowledge of God and of Christ. Peter is therefore praying that "grace," the divine source of all blessings, and
"peace," the deepest experience of the soul, may be increased, by and in this knowledge; and he prays with confidence, knowing that, or "seeing that," the "divine power"
of God "hath granted unto us all things that pertain unto
life and godliness," through this knowledge, which is here
defined as a knowledge of Christ "that called us by his
own glory and virtue." All that we need for the nurture
of spiritual life and for the development of godliness has
been given to us in our knowledge of Christ who has at-
tracted us to be his followers by the manifestation of his
own moral excellence and goodness. These excellences
of their Lord awake in believers a hope of attaining to his
likeness, they assure them of the certain enjoyment of all
the pardon and peace and future blessedness of which the
Savior has spoken, even "his precious and exceeding great
promises," including his glorious return to which this
epistle continually refers. It is the purpose of God that,
through a knowledge of these promises and by cherishing
them in faith, we may not only escape the moral corruption

and decay which pervade the world because of evil desires and perverted passions, but that also we may attain to his likeness, developing more and more of his holiness and purity and love, being "transformed" into his image by the power of his indwelling Spirit.

b. *The Exhortation: The Growth of Knowledge*
Ch. 1:5-11

5 Yea, and for this very cause adding on your part all diligence, in your faith supply virtue; and in your virtue knowledge; 6 and in your knowledge self-control; and in your self-control patience; and in your patience godliness; 7 and in your godliness brotherly kindness; and in your brotherly kindness love. 8 For if these things are yours and abound, they make you to be not idle nor unfruitful unto the knowledge of our Lord Jesus Christ. 9 For he that lacketh these things is blind, seeing only what is near, having forgotten the cleansing from his old sins. 10 Wherefore, brethren, give the more diligence to make your calling and election sure: for if ye do these things, ye shall never stumble: 11 for thus shall be richly supplied unto you the entrance into the eternal kingdom of our Lord and Saviour Jesus Christ.

In view of the faith which God has graciously given, in view of the knowledge of Christ which they possess, in view of the fact that they are "partakers of the divine nature," the readers are now urged to strive for such growth in Christian virtues, for such a development of spiritual graces, that their knowledge and faith shall be "not idle nor unfruitful." The suggestion seems to be that knowledge will thus be increased, that knowing will come by doing; that the condition of receiving more light is a faithful use of the light one has; that strenuous exercise of Christian graces results in a fuller comprehension of spiritual truth.

In the beautiful list of graces which Peter here exhibits, each grace apparently grows out of the preceding grace, and in turn becomes the soil or atmosphere in which the next is nourished, while all are rooted in "faith." Nevertheless, the growth is not spontaneous; on our part there is demanded the expenditure of toil and effort. God has granted us the new life; but like a divine germ it needs to be developed by the earnest care which we are to "bring in by the side of" the divine gift; we are to add on our part "all diligence"; progress in Christian living is made only by cooperation of the human will with the divine.

"In your faith supply virtue"; this is not the same as "add to your faith virtue"; but, as above suggested, "with and by your faith supply virtue"; "faith" is the source and gives the power by which "virtue" is to be developed; "faith without works is dead," but it shows itself to be living and real when it produces "moral excellence"; real trust in Christ and true belief in him will always issue in right conduct, or "virtue."

So "virtue" in turn is to develop "knowledge," which here means "practical skill in the details of Christian duty" rather than the knowledge of God and of Christ which in the previous section were used very much in the sense of "faith." "And in your knowledge [supply] self-control," according to which, in all the experiences of life, reason governs passion; "and in your self-control patience," or "endurance," for while "self-control" enables one to curb his desires, patience gives him power steadfastly to endure evils which press upon him from without; "and in your patience godliness," which characterizes the life of one who continually lives "as seeing him who is invisible"; "and in your godliness brotherly kindness," or affection for fellow Christians, "and in your brotherly kindness love" for Christ and the whole world. The relation of these seven virtues has been thus stated: "Faith is the gift of God already received; to this must be added (1) moral strength which enables a man to do what he knows to be right; (2) spiritual discernment; (3) self-control by which a man resists temptation; (4) endurance by which he bears up under persecution or adversity; (5) right feeling and behavior toward God, and (6) toward the brethren, and (7) toward all."

To the patient development of these virtues we are encouraged by the assurance, which forms the main burden of this paragraph, that where these are possessed and are increasing, there one is not idle or unfruitful in the attainment of knowledge; a diligent practice of Christian virtues always increases spiritual insight.   On the other hand their absence or neglect produces, or constitutes, spiritual blindness or nearsightedness: "For he that lacketh these things is blind, seeing only what is near."   It is true that the reason why things unseen and eternal seem to us so unreal is that we are making so little effort toward moral and spiritual progress.   This lack of spiritual perception may extend so far that one may forget "the cleansing from his old sins," may actually become oblivious of the pardon and cleansing in which his Christian life began, and of all that God has done for him.

"Wherefore, brethren," in view of the possible increase and the possible loss of "knowledge," and so of the "salvation" it involves, "give the more diligence to make your calling and election sure."   The divine choice and call do not make human effort unnecessary.   If, however, the Christian graces are being developed, and knowledge is enlarging, "If ye do these things, ye shall never stumble." This does not mean that the Christian will never sin, but that such patient effort toward progress will safeguard him against faults and failings, and will assure the completion of his journey to the heavenly city; he will indeed be richly provided for "the entrance into the eternal kingdom of our Lord and Saviour Jesus Christ."

c. The Promise: The Grounds of Knowledge   Ch. 1:12-21

12 Wherefore I shall be ready always to put you in remembrance of these things, though ye know them, and are established in the truth which is with you.   13 And I think

*it right, as long as I am in this tabernacle, to stir you up by putting you in remembrance; 14 knowing that the putting off of my tabernacle cometh swiftly, even as our Lord Jesus Christ signified unto me. 15 Yea, I will give diligence that at every time ye may be able after my decease to call these things to remembrance. 16 For we did not follow cunningly devised fables, when we made known unto you the power and coming of our Lord Jesus Christ, but we were eyewitnesses of his majesty. 17 For he received from God the Father honor and glory, when there was borne such a voice to him by the Majestic Glory, This is my beloved Son, in whom I am well pleased: 18 and this voice we our-*selves *heard borne out of heaven, when we were with him in the holy mount. 19 And we have the word of prophecy* made *more sure; whereunto ye do well that ye take heed, as unto a lamp shining in a dark place, until the day dawn, and the day-star arise in your hearts: 20 knowing this first, that no prophecy of scripture is of private interpretation. 21 For no prophecy ever came by the will of man: but men spake from God, being moved by the Holy Spirit.*

Peter, in opening his epistle, has shown that in the knowledge of Christ has been given all that is needed for "life and godliness"; he has urged an increase of this knowledge by the development of Christian virtues that so may be provided an entrance into the heavenly Kingdom; he now promises to aid his readers to keep these truths in mind and assures them that their knowledge is well supported by the testimony of inspired apostles and prophets.

Thus he does not propose to teach new truths, but declares that he will "be ready always" to put his readers in remembrance of the truth in which they are already established. He regards this as his duty and more especially because his own death is approaching, or, as he says "the putting off of my tabernacle cometh swiftly"; his body is like a tent which his spirit is soon to leave. He is sure of this because he is now far advanced in years, and his Lord had told him that, when old, he should die a martyr's death. Here Peter even promises to make provision that after his death his readers shall be able "to call these things to remembrance"; just how he proposed to fulfill this promise he does not say—probably by writing other letters; but some have conjectured that he meant to appoint teachers, or even that he referred to the Gospel of Mark, which is thought to have been written under his direction.

The climax and inspiring center of all the truth Peter so prized concerned the personal, visible return of Christ. This was the great motive for holy living to which he constantly appealed in his First Epistle; this was the doctrine ridiculed and opposed by the false teachers whom this Second Epistle was written to rebuke. Peter declares that, in his statements concerning the divine power and future coming of Christ, he and his fellow apostles did "not follow cunningly devised fables," but they spoke as men who, with their own eyes, had seen the "majesty," the radiant splendor, the heavenly glory, in which Christ would reappear. This vision was granted to them on the Mount of Transfiguration when Jesus "received from God the Father honor and glory, when there was borne such a voice to him by the Majestic Glory, [that is, by God himself], This is my beloved Son, in whom I am well pleased." This transfiguration scene was a foregleam, a part, a manifestation, and so a proof, of the majesty and splendor in which Christ would appear when he returned in his own glory and that of the Father and that of the holy angels. This experience confirmed the word of the prophets; it has made it an even firmer ground of confidence; previously the assurance came by faith, but now that in the transfiguration there has been granted a specimen of the coming glory, sight has made assurance doubly sure: "We have the word of prophecy made more sure; whereunto ye do well that ye take heed, as unto a lamp shining in a dark place." In this dusk and dimly lighted world, in all its mystery of confusing events, prophecy shines forth as a lamp, the only lamp we have to guide us. We must give heed to it "until the day dawn, and the day-star arise." Thus (according to Tregelles, Schott, and others) it may be best to punctuate this last clause: "Ye do well that ye take heed, in your hearts, until the day dawn"; that is while the shadows hang so heavily upon the present world you do well to take earnest heed to the light of prophecy, until at last the Lord returns and the shadows flee away. If, however, we accept the usual punctuation, the meaning may be that we should take heed of prophecy and ponder its statements, until in our hearts there dawns a bright and confident expectation of the coming of Christ.

To such earnest heed of prophecy we are specially encouraged by the consideration that "no prophecy of scripture is of private interpretation," or, probably "of private origination," that is, it does not come from the prophets' own interpretation of the future; "for no prophecy" as Peter adds, "ever came by the will of man: but men spake from God, being moved by the Holy Spirit." Therefore, upon the testimony of apostles who were eyewitnesses, upon the words of prophets who were divinely inspired, rest our saving knowledge of Christ and our hope of his glorious return.

II
THE TEACHERS OF ERROR

a. Their Punishment   Ch. 2:1-9

1 But there arose false prophets also among the people, as among you also there shall be false teachers, who shall privily bring in destructive heresies, denying even the Master that bought them, bringing upon themselves swift destruction. 2 And many shall follow their lascivious doings; by reason of whom the way of the truth shall be evil spoken of. 3 And in covetousness shall they with feigned words make merchandise of you: whose sentence now from of old lingereth not, and their destruction slumbereth not. 4 For if God spared not angels when they sinned, but cast them down to hell, and committed them to pits of darkness, to be reserved unto judgment; 5 and spared not the ancient world, but preserved Noah with seven others, a preacher of righteousness, when he brought a flood upon the world of the ungodly; 6 and turning the cities of Sodom and Gomorrah into ashes condemned them with an overthrow, having made them an example unto those that should live ungodly; 7 and delivered righteous Lot, sore distressed by the lascivious life of the wicked 8 (for that righteous man dwelling among them, in seeing and hearing, vexed his righteous soul from day to day with their lawless deeds): 9 the Lord knoweth how to deliver the godly out of temptation, and to keep the unrighteous under punishment unto the day of judgment.

Peter had just assured his readers that inspired prophets, in their teaching, had given them a lamp which they should cherish and use in the prevailing darkness, until the Lord return. He now reminds them that of old there were "false prophets" as well as true, and that, similarly, in the Christian church there are "false teachers" as well as inspired apostles, and that such teachers will appear in all ages until Christ reappears. The mention of these teachers brings Peter to the very heart of his epistle, which is mainly designed to warn his readers against these authors of destructive heresies and to defend the truth concerning the return of Christ, which, in particular, was being denied.

As the chapter opens, Peter declares that these false leaders are doomed to certain punishment; they are "bringing upon themselves swift destruction"; their sentence "from of old lingereth not, and their destruction slumbereth not," it had been predicted in other days, of similar men, and it is no dead letter but soon will be executed upon them. Their conduct is described as "denying even the Master that bought them," as by their impure lives and their corruption of his teachings they actually disclaimed and renounced the Lord and Master who had died for them. As a result of their influence, "many shall follow their lascivious doings; by reason of whom the way of the truth shall be evil spoken of," while the teachers enrich themselves by the money they extort from their victims.

Thus the first four verses describe the doom, the conduct, and the influence of these men, and so outline and summarize the whole chapter. This chapter, it will be remembered, is closely paralleled by the Epistle of Jude. The supposition is that one writer borrowed from the other or both from a common source. It should be noted however, that when Jude gives examples of the certain punishment of the wicked he makes no mention of the deliverance of the righteous. Peter, however, uses three illustrations of certain doom, but in two of these he lays great stress upon the fact that "the Lord knoweth how to deliver the godly out of temptation, and to keep the unrighteous under punishment unto the day of judgment." Of these examples of punishment the first is that of the fallen angels; the nature of their sin is not mentioned, but it is elsewhere suggested as having been caused by pride. The second is that of the world before the flood, the special feature of which was disobedience to God. The third is that of the destruction of Sodom and Gomorrah; the guilt of these cities was that of moral impurity. Thus Peter pictures the certain punishment of the false teachers, but he also paints their character, and intimates their pride, rebellion, and sensuality. He also intimates, however, that even though the righteous are few in number, as Noah and his family, or as Lot in lawless Sodom, God is certain to deliver those who trust and serve him. His words are designed to comfort and encourage believers in the darkest days of heresy and false teaching and impending judgments: "The Lord knoweth how to deliver the godly out of temptation."

b. Their Character and Conduct Ch. 2:10-16

10 But chiefly them that walk after the flesh in the lust of defilement, and despise dominion. Daring, self-willed, they tremble not to rail at dignities: 11 whereas angels, though greater in might and power, bring not a railing judgment against them before the Lord. 12 But these, as creatures without reason, born mere animals to be taken and destroyed, railing in matters whereof they are ignorant, shall in their destroying surely be destroyed, 13 suffering wrong as the hire of wrong-doing; men that count it pleasure to revel in the day-time, spots and blemishes, revelling in their deceivings while they feast with you; 14 having eyes full of adultery, and that cannot cease from sin; enticing unstedfast souls; having a heart exercised in covetousness; children of cursing; 15 forsaking the right way, they went astray, having followed the way of Balaam the son of Beor, who loved the hire of wrong-doing; 16 but he was rebuked for his own transgression: a dumb ass spake with man's voice and stayed the madness of the prophet.

Peter has already announced the doom and briefly designated the teachers of error who were corrupting the

Christian church; he now paints their character and conduct in vivid and forbidding colors. The two paragraphs
are inseparably interwoven, the description of punishment
and of sin. Thus when he mentions "chiefly them that
walk after the flesh in the lust of defilement," he means
that they, more obviously than other sinners, are kept under the judgment of God, and he specifies their character
as walking "after the flesh," making lust their law, and
further, he states, they "despise dominion," looking with
contempt upon the power and majesty of the Lord. Naturally therefore, "daring, self-willed, they tremble not to rail
at dignities," but treat with abuse the lawful rulers of the
church. Such daring presumption is rebuked by the example of angels who refrain from insulting and condemning beings less powerful than themselves. These teachers
are like "animals," without reason, mere brute beasts making a pretense of knowledge, and they are certain to be
punished for their wrongdoing, as they deserve. Their
idea of pleasure is wanton living, in open daylight. They
are "spots and blemishes" in the church which should be
pure and holy. Their eyes betray their adulterous
thoughts, never satisfied with sin. They allure and corrupt unsteady, unstable, "unstedfast souls." "Children of
cursing" that they are, they have left the straight path,
wandering away from it by following the way of Balaam;
he, like these false teachers, "loved the hire of wrong-
doing"; he wished the gold Balak offered and desired to
curse Israel contrary to God's command; he was "rebuked" for his breach of law, when his dumb ass, acting
contrary to law of another kind, spoke with human voice
and resisted the mad infatuation of the prophet.

Like Balaam of old, men who try to serve God and gold,
and false teachers, such as Peter describes, who hide their
covetousness and impurity under the cloak of Christian
profession, are doomed to moral blindness, to disappointment, to disgrace, and to death.

c. Their Evil Influence   Ch. 2:17-22

> 17 These are springs without water, and mists driven by
> a storm; for whom the blackness of darkness hath been re-
> served. 18 For, uttering great swelling words of vanity,
> they entice in the lusts of the flesh, by lasciviousness, those
> who are just escaping from them that live in error;   19
> promising them liberty, while they themselves are bond-
> servants of corruption; for of whom a man is overcome,
> of the same is he also brought into bondage. 20 For if,
> after they have escaped the defilements of the world through
> the knowledge of the Lord and Saviour Jesus Christ, they
> are again entangled therein and overcome, the last state is
> become worse with them than the first. 21 For it were bet-
> ter for them not to have known the way of righteousness,
> than, after knowing it, to turn back from the holy com-
> mandment delivered unto them. 22 It has happened unto
> them according to the true proverb, The dog turning to his
> own vomit again, and the sow that had washed to wallow-
> ing in the mire.

The most distressing feature in the picture of the teachers of error whom Peter is denouncing in this present chapter is that of their influence upon the members of the
church. The pitiful fact is that such men secure a following; they know enough of truth, and can employ sufficient
pious phrases, to beguile and entrap weak and unsuspect-
ing souls. They profess to be sources of spiritual help;
how different they are, in reality! "These are springs without water"; what a disappointment to those who are thirst-
ing! These are "mists driven by a storm"; mists might
supply some moisture, or protect from the burning sun,
but when driven by the wind, as these teachers by their
passions, they can only blind and distress.

In contrast with all their boastful pretense, "uttering
great swelling words of vanity," they lead astray, by offers
of sensual indulgence, those who are just escaping from
sinful companions and practices. They teach that as a
Christian is "free from the law" he can live in license, and

can show his liberty by indulging in sin. The fact is that such teachers are themselves the slaves of sin, while they are promising freedom to others; "for a man is the slave of whatever overpowers him." Most pitiful of all is the case of those who are misled, and who under such influences renounce their allegiance to Christ: "For if after they have escaped the defilements of the world through the knowledge of the Lord and Saviour Jesus Christ, they are again entangled therein and overcome, the last state is become worse with them than the first." In these and the closing words of the chapter a solemn warning is sounded both for the teachers of error and their followers. "For it were better for them not to have known the way of righteousness, than, after knowing it, to turn back from the holy commandment." It is useless, and quite aside from the purpose of Peter, to argue here either against or for the doctrine of "the perseverance of the saints" or the possibility of "falling from grace." From the proverb with which the chapter closes it would seem that the persons described had never really experienced a "new birth" or a change of nature; however, the point here is to warn persons against self-deception, against all false sense of security, against false teachers who make light of sin and corrupt the teachings of Christ. No one can presume upon a past religious experience, whether it was real or imaginary. Each one must, and will, increase his knowledge of Christ by a diligent cultivation of Christian graces in case he is to find an "entrance into the eternal kingdom."

III
THE COMING OF CHRIST

Ch. 3

a. The Certainty Ch. 3:1-7

*1 This is now, beloved, the second epistle that I write
unto you; and in both of them I stir up your sincere mind
by putting you in remembrance; 2 that ye should remember the words which were spoken before by the holy prophets, and the commandment of the Lord and Saviour
through your apostles: 3 knowing this first, that in the
last days mockers shall come with mockery, walking after
their own lusts, 4 and saying, Where is the promise of his
coming? for, from the day that the fathers fell asleep, all
things continue as they were from the beginning of the
creation. 5 For this they wilfully forget, that there were
heavens from of old, and an earth compacted out of water
and amidst water, by the word of God; 6 by which means
the world that then was, being overflowed with water, perished: 7 but the heavens that now are, and the earth, by
the same word have been stored up for fire, being reserved
against the day of judgment and destruction of ungodly
men.*

The return of Christ and the establishment on earth of
his perfected Kingdom has been the blessed hope of the
church through all the passing centuries. In writing his
First Epistle, this hope was continually used by Peter as an
inspiring motive for patience in suffering and for fidelity
in the performance of duty. In this Second Epistle, the
same truth also is so continually in mind that the two letters have commonly been called the "Epistles of Hope."

Thus as he begins this third chapter, Peter states that his
purpose in writing is to remind his readers of the teachings
of apostles and prophets concerning the return of Christ,

and specifically of their prediction that, as the present age drew to its close, men would appear who would ridicule the very idea of a second advent: "knowing this first, that in the last days mockers shall come with mockery, walking after their own lusts, and saying, Where is the promise of his coming?" As their appearance had been predicted thus in connection with the Lord's return, the very existence and words of such scoffers proved the truth which they attempted to deny.

It may be noted that there is a very modern accent in the two grounds on which their denial is based: first, the lapse of time since the promise was made; and second, the improbability of its fulfillment: "for, from the day that the fathers fell asleep, all things continue as they were from the beginning of the creation." That is to say, first, our Lord had suggested that his return might be at an early date, and now practically a generation had passed away, at least most of the early fathers of the church were dead, and as Christ had not returned there must be some mistake about his promise or the common interpretation of his promise; he had not come, so, the scoffers concluded, he would not come.

The second objection sounds quite as familiar today: "all things continue as they were from the beginning of the creation"; that is to say, law is uniform, miracle is impossible, the sole process in the universe is evolution, the supernatural is inconceivable; the return of Christ with its attendant circumstances is absolutely miraculous, catastrophic, supernatural; therefore it is the foolish dream of fanatics and not worthy the serious thought of men of enlightenment and culture.

This second objection Peter at once discusses; the first he meets in the next paragraph. As to the "uniformity of nature," is it true that there has been no divine act, no "supernatural intervention?" Do not these scoffers "wilfully forget" and stubbornly neglect certain known facts? How did the world come into being, and how was the "process of evolution" begun; were these not "by the word of God?" Or, how about the flood? was it not by this same divine Word that "the world . . . being overflowed with water, perished?" If God sent a deluge to punish a guilty world, is it not possible that Christ may appear in flaming fire to punish the ungodly and to deliver his saints?

This seems to be the argument of Peter. Of course his language is figurative. It is certain that the flood did not destroy the heaven and the earth; of this absurd statement Peter is guilty if words must be taken literally. So when Christ comes he will not destroy the earth. Fire is a symbol of divine judgment and of purification. Just what the figures of speech imply will always be a matter of controversy and conjecture; but as to the fact of our Lord's return there need be no doubt. It is established, as Peter declares, by the words of "the holy prophets" and of "the Lord and Saviour" himself. These words must be studied with patience, and expounded with care, and defended with charity; but in days of deepest darkness they are, to men of "sincere mind" and simple faith, stars of hope, pointing to the dawn and the glorious appearing of the King.

b. The Time and Circumstances   Ch. 3:8-13

8 But forget not this one thing, beloved, that one day is with the Lord as a thousand years, and a thousand years as one day. 9 The Lord is not slack concerning his promise, as some count slackness; but is longsuffering to you-ward, not wishing that any should perish, but that all should come to repentance. 10 But the day of the Lord will come as a thief; in the which the heavens shall pass away with a great noise, and the elements shall be dissolved with fervent heat, and the earth and the works that are therein shall be burned up. 11 Seeing that these things are thus all to be dissolved, what manner of persons ought ye to be in all holy living and godliness, 12 looking for and earnestly desiring the

coming of the day of God, by reason of which the heavens being on fire shall be dissolved, and the elements shall melt with fervent heat? 13 But, according to his promise, we look for new heavens and a new earth, wherein dwelleth righteousness.

While the blessed hope of their Lord's return has been the stay and comfort of his followers in every age, there have always been men, even within the church, who have ridiculed the doctrine as an idle fancy, a chimera, a dream. There were such men in the days of Peter, and he writes his Second Epistle to warn his readers against these teachers of unbelief; such teachers exist today, and express polite surprise that any persons could be so lacking in intelligence as to expect a literal, visible, glorious reappearing of Jesus Christ; such have been predicted to appear "in the last days," and their scoffing will make them unconscious witnesses of the fact they deride.

In the earlier verses of this chapter, Peter has indicated that such unbelief was not due to any lack of prediction on the part of Christ or of the prophets and apostles, but was due to the long delay in the fulfillment of the promises: no one who reads the New Testament questions the fact that the early Christians expected the return of the Lord, and regarded it as possible in their own day; "but," say these doubters, "the early Church was evidently mistaken; the prediction has been discredited by these ages of delay." To such, Peter makes his memorable reply: "But forget not this one thing, beloved, that one day is with the Lord as a thousand years, and a thousand years as one day." That is to say, time is purely relative, and what seems a long delay to man is not long in the mind of the Eternal; to him the issues of a single day are permanent, endless; and the events of a thousand years are present, real, already passing before him.

Thus to the charge of a long delay, Peter replies, first, that men are poor judges of the length and shortness of time in which divine counsels are concerned; he replies, in the next place, that what, even in human judgment, is a long delay is occasioned by a wise and gracious purpose: "The Lord is not slack concerning his promise," not unmindful, not indifferent to his word, "but is longsuffering to you ward, not wishing that any should perish, but that all should come to repentance"; if he delays his judgment, it is that men, even the readers of this epistle, may have time to repent and to accept the salvation he has provided in Jesus Christ.

In the third place, Peter states that the long delay should not make men careless or lull them into a false security, for "the day of the Lord will come as a thief." The mere fact that events seem to be taking their usual course, or have so continued for ages, is no proof that the Lord will not return. By the world the event will be unexpected; the time is always uncertain; the lack of expectation on the part of believers is a predicted sign that the coming may be near.

It is folly to "set the time" for the Lord's return, or to extort from some obscure passages of Scripture a prediction of the exact date of his coming; nevertheless there are certain events and circumstances which will serve as signs for those who are watchful. "Ye . . . are not in darkness, that that day should overtake you as a thief," wrote Paul to the Thessalonian believers. Of these circumstances Peter mentions only the physical convulsions which precede and attend the appearing of Christ. The language he employs is highly figurative and when taken literally leads to strange conclusions. He borrows his figures from the last two chapters of Isaiah and from the Eighteenth Psalm; the latter is describing a severe storm, as it declares that "the foundations of the world were laid bare"; so Peter declares, "The earth and the works that are therein shall be discovered" [margin]. Isaiah described the blessedness of the return from captivity, that was to be, for the Jews, like enjoying "new heavens and a new earth." In no case does it mean that the coming of the Lord is to destroy this earth. When Peter declares that "the heavens shall pass away with a great noise, and the elements shall be dissolved with fervent heat, and the earth and the works that are therein shall be burned up" he is merely referring to the "signs" attending the coming of Christ to which the Master himself referred when he said: "The sun shall be darkened, and the moon shall not give her light, and the stars shall be falling from heaven, and the powers that are in the heavens shall be shaken. And then shall they see the Son of man coming in clouds with great power and glory." "But when these things begin to come to pass, look up, and lift up your heads; because your redemption draweth nigh." Peter is merely giving a picture of coming judgments. The issue of these convulsions, whatever their nature, is "new heavens and a new earth, wherein dwelleth righteousness"; not a new globe, for the nations of the world are pictured as still here; as in Isaiah and the two closing chapters of the Bible, the "new earth" is this same old world, purified, glorified, redeemed, and the scene of righteousness and blessedness and universal peace.

c. The Consequent Exhortations   Ch. 3:14-18

14 Wherefore, beloved, seeing that ye look for these things, give diligence that ye may be found in peace, without spot and blameless in his sight. 15 And account that the longsuffering of our Lord is salvation; even as our beloved brother Paul also, according to the wisdom given to him, wrote unto you; 16 as also in all his epistles, speaking in them of these things: wherein are some things hard to be understood, which the ignorant and unstedfast wrest, as they do also the other scriptures, unto their own destruction. 17 Ye therefore, beloved, knowing these things beforehand, beware lest, being carried away with the error of the wicked, ye fall from your own stedfastness. 18 But grow in the grace and knowledge of our Lord and Saviour Jesus Christ. To him be the glory both now and for ever. Amen.

The purpose of Peter is intensely practical. He has written of the return of Christ not to arouse idle speculation or to occasion bitter disputes but to make better men and women. Two facts he makes perfectly clear: Christ will come, the result will be a reign of righteousness. But as the coming is attended with judgment, "what manner of persons" ought we to be "in all holy living and godliness"? Should we not be "looking for and earnestly desiring the coming of the day of God"? Thus Peter argues. We may not be able to interpret all his symbols, or to understand all that the "day of God" will contain, but the exhortations of the apostle are clear; he makes our duty plain.

Thus, as he brings the epistle to a close, Peter gives two parting injunctions: one is to steadfastness, the other to spiritual growth. "Wherefore, beloved, seeing that ye look for these things, give diligence that ye may be found in peace"; the return of Christ should not occasion restless excitement but calm confidence; it should impel us to lives of purity that we may be "without spot and blameless in his sight," for if we are expecting the bridegroom we should keep our garments white and clean. We should remember that if he delays his coming it is to give us an opportunity to accept and to proclaim his salvation, even as Paul has written in his epistles; these epistles are inspired and to be accepted as holy Scripture, but they contain passages hard to understand which men who are ignorant of spiritual truth and eager to find an excuse for sin have misinterpreted so as to allow themselves license which is destroying their souls. We have been warned in advance of the evil influences of false teachers, and of the peril of turning from the truth; we therefore should stand firm and steadfast. We should "grow in the grace and knowledge of our Lord and Saviour Jesus Christ." This can be possible, as Peter has shown us, only by daily and diligently developing the virtues which we have seen revealed in our Lord, and by continually dwelling upon his word. "To him be the glory both now and for ever. Amen."

THE FIRST EPISTLE OF JOHN

THE FIRST EPISTLE
OF JOHN

Are you certain that you are a Christian? Are you conscious of fellowship with the Father and with his Son? Are you confident that by faith in Christ you have been "born again" and that you are a true "child of God"? To answer such questions this epistle was composed. The writer states his purpose quite clearly: "These things have I written unto you, that ye may know that ye have eternal life, even unto you that believe on the name of the Son of God." The phrase "eternal life" does not mean merely endless existence; it denotes not only the length, but also the kind, of life; it suggests a relation, not to time, but to God; it describes the life revealed in Christ and shared by those who put their trust in him.

The assurance that one has this "life" is not mystical or mysterious. The knowledge is based upon grounds which are simple and plain. They are chiefly three: faith and righteousness and love. They correspond to three great affirmations in reference to God made by the writer: "God is light," "He is righteous," "God is love." If such is the nature of the Father, then his children will be like him; they will believe in his Son who is "the light of the world"; they will be righteous "even as he is righteous"; they will "love the children of God"; and they will "love God and do his commandments." Thus belief and righteousness and love are declared to be tests of "eternal life." They can be absent from the experience of no real Christian.

The epistle, however, is much more than a mere series of tests. So conscious are we of the imperfection of our faith and holiness and love, that such tests might be ap-

plied in such a way as to tease and torment the truest follower of Christ. The writer aims to comfort and to encourage. He wishes to assure the humblest believers that
"eternal life" is their present possession, and to urge them
to manifest more and more fully its characteristics and its
qualities. These "tests of life" are not intended to gratify
morbid introspection, nor to encourage our self-righteous-
ness, nor to enable us to criticize and condemn others.
The purpose of the letter is to give to believers a happy
confidence in their blessed state, to enable them to appre-
ciate their marvelous privileges, and to encourage them
to a faithful performance of their duties, to a fuller development of life, and to a more perfect fellowship with God.

The writer has another purpose, closely related and
equally practical: he desires to warn his readers against
certain prevalent errors of belief and practice. There were
those who once had been professed Christians, who "went
out" from the church, who denied that our Lord is truly
God and truly man, at once human and divine. To this
false teaching they apparently added the perilous doctrine
that one who was living in sin might still be "spiritual" and
a "child of God." So dangerous were such teachers, so
truly hostile to Christianity, that the writer calls them
"antichrists" and declares that they have no fellowship
with the Father or the Son. They are not "of God"; they
are "of the world."

This little word "of" is quite significant. Like "in," it
is one of the most important words of the epistle. "Of"
denotes origin, nature, source, likeness, birth; thus, one
who is "of God" is born of God, is like God, is a child
of God. "In" signifies "union with," permanent indwelling, "fellowship"; thus, as believers in Christ, we are urged
to "abide in him," and are assured that "we are in him
that is true."

These little words, used in connection with such leading
terms as "God" and "the world," "light and darkness,"
"love" and "hate," aid in forming the striking contrasts

which characterize the epistle, and, as already intimated, they summarize in large measure the content of the epistle which concerns the life of those who are described either as "in him," and so having fellowship with God, or as "of God" and so "children of God." The style of the epistle is pure, clear, and artlessly simple. Its profound truths are set forth in brief phrases, and are emphasized by repetitions which in form are rhythmic and poetic. Its unity is apparent, yet the structure is such as to evade exact analysis. The main truths and something of their relation may be indicated by the appended outline. It is suggested in part by a modern writer whose interpretations mold in large measure the exposition which follows:

1. Introduction: The Life Eternal Revealed in Christ
   I John 1:1-4
2. The Life of Fellowship with God   *Chs. 1:5 to 2:29*
   a. Tested by Righteousness   *Chs. 1:5 to 2:6*
   b. Tested by Love   *Ch. 2:7-17*
   c. Tested by Belief   *Ch. 2:18-29*
3. The Life of the Children of God   *Chs. 3:1 to 4:6*
   a. Tested by Righteousness   *Ch. 3:1-10*
   b. Tested by Love   *Ch. 3:11-24*
   c. Tested by Belief   *Ch. 4:1-6*
4. The Source of Love   *Ch. 4:7-21*
5. The Triumph of Righteousness   *Ch. 5:1-5*
6. The Grounds of Belief   *Ch. 5:6-12*
7. Conclusion: Christian Certainties   *Ch. 5:13-21*

I

THE LIFE ETERNAL REVEALED IN CHRIST

I John 1:1-4

1 That which was from the beginning, that which we have heard, that which we have seen with our eyes, that which we beheld, and our hands handled, concerning the Word of life 2 (and the life was manifested, and we have seen, and bear witness, and declare unto you the life, the eternal life, which was with the Father, and was manifested unto us); 3 that which we have seen and heard declare we unto you also, that ye also may have fellowship with us: yea, and our fellowship is with the Father, and with his Son Jesus Christ: 4 and these things we write, that our joy may be made full.

The writer of this epistle makes no mention of his name; but when we compare these opening sentences with those of the Gospel of John we are struck with the similarity; and as we read on, in both compositions, we find the same phrases, the same profound thoughts, the same unique style, the same spiritual insight, until we conclude that the author of this epistle, almost beyond question, is the "disciple whom Jesus loved," John, the son of Zebedee, the brother of James. He is an old man now. His imprisonment on the lonely isle of Patmos is past, and he is probably residing in Ephesus, caring for the churches, and revered as the last surviving member of the band of apostles. It is this consciousness of his peculiar relation to Christ which gives to his epistle its prevailing note of authority. The writer is full of tenderness and affection, yet his quiet words are delivered with an implication that they are infallible and final, and that from them there can be no appeal. Apostolic authority is nowhere claimed; it is everywhere assumed. It is helpful to believe that we are reading the inspired words of the man who was the most intimate and beloved companion of our Lord in the days of his earthly ministry.

Nor are the readers specified or described. Of all the "general" or "catholic" epistles, this epistle is most obviously written for Christians in "general," for believers in the "whole world." That it is written to Christians is continually implied, and is definitely stated: "These things have I written unto you . . . that believe on the name of the Son of God." No matter in what city or province they may have lived to whom these lines first came, it is evident that their message comes as a personal appeal to believers in every land and age.

The theme at once arrests attention. It is life, or more definitely, eternal life. The term denotes not merely endless existence, but the life of God, revealed in Jesus Christ, and shared by all who put their trust in him. This does not mean that believers become "divine" or partake of the being of God, but they do possess a new moral life; its source is in God, its channel is faith, its issues are goodness and love. So inseparable is this life from Christ, that he is called "the Word of life." In him was manifested that life which was timeless and which he possessed in eternal fellowship with the Father. That which the apostles have known of this life "from the beginning," that which they "have heard," that which they "have seen" with their eyes, that which they "beheld" and their "hands handled," that is to form the burden of this matchless letter of life.

The purpose of the epistle is that, by a knowledge of the life revealed, the readers may have fellowship with the apostles in their assurance as partakers of this life, in their appreciation of its privileges, in their accomplishment of its duties. The fellowship which the apostles enjoy is more than mere human companionship and intimacy, it is a fellowship "with the Father, and with his Son Jesus Christ." To promote and perfect such fellowship, the writer declares, will make his joy full and complete.

We should note then that in his introduction John makes plain the fact that life, true life, eternal life, consists in fellowship with God. This is the highest possible experience for the human soul.

Further, he shows that this fellowship is possible only through faith in Christ, who is himself the Manifestation of the life of God, or as John calls him, "the Word of life."

Again John declares this Christ to be divine and human; even "from the beginning" he has been in timeless, vital relation with the Father, but he has been revealed as truly man who could be seen and heard. He is a risen Christ, for John refers to his being "handled" in language which reminds us definitely of the scene in that upper room at the close of the resurrection day.

We are further reminded that faith in this Christ is not a matter of credulity or mysticism or superstition. Faith is belief founded upon evidence. The apostles were men of reason, they had the witness of their senses, they had abundant opportunity for investigating the facts. They testified that which they had seen and heard. There is an interesting climax in the order of the expressions used by John; they heard what was at a distance, they saw what was nearer, they beheld what was closer still, their "hands handled" the divine Lord who stood in their midst. So too, for such as follow him, the divine Christ becomes ever more real as they find in him eternal life and fellowship with God.

Further still, we may note that the highest fellowship among men is that which comes from accepting Christian verities. No other communion is so intimate, and no other companionships so inspiring as those which are based on a vital faith in Christ.

Finally we may note that the deepest source of joy is found in service, and the highest form of service consists in bringing others into fellowship "with the Father, and with his Son Jesus Christ." By such service "our joy may be made full."

II
THE LIFE OF FELLOWSHIP WITH GOD
Chs. 1:5 to 2:29

a. Tested by Righteousness   Chs. 1:5 to 2:6

5 And this is the message which we have heard from him and announce unto you, that God is light, and in him is no darkness at all. 6 If we say that we have fellowship with him and walk in the darkness, we lie, and do not the truth: 7 but if we walk in the light, as he is in he light, we have fellowship one with another, and the blood of Jesus his Son cleanseth us from all sin. 8 If we say that we have no sin, we deceive ourselves, and the truth is not in us. 9 If we confess our sins, he is faithful and righteous to forgive us our sins, and to cleanse us from all unrighteousness. 10 If we say that we have not sinned, we make him a liar, and his word is not in us.

1 My little children, these things write I unto you that ye may not sin. And if any man sin, we have an Advocate with the Father, Jesus Christ the righteous: 2 and he is the propitiation for our sins; and not for ours only, but also for the whole world. 3 And hereby we know that we know him, if we keep his commandments. 4 He that saith, I know him, and keepeth not his commandments, is a liar, and the truth is not in him; 5 but whoso keepeth his word, in him verily hath the love of God been perfected. Hereby we know that we are in him: 6 he that saith he abideth in him ought himself also to walk even as he walked.

In the opening verses of his epistle, John has described the Christian life as resulting from a knowledge of God as he is revealed in Christ, and as consisting essentially in fellowship with God. In the later portions of the epistle, this life is otherwise described as issuing from a new birth as the result of which believers become the children of God. Here, however, and through the first two chapters of the letter, the "eternal life" which is possessed by Christians is regarded as a divine fellowship.

In accordance with his purpose, John at once suggests the tests of this life. If one has fellowship with God, he will have accepted all that God has revealed in Christ, and will be living in accord with this revelation. He will be like God; but what is God like? "God is light." This great truth underlies all that the first two chapters contain. Light is the most beautiful, the most glorious, thing in the world. It is the symbol of purity and love and truth. The main function of light, however, is to reveal, and the writer has in mind mainly the self-revelation of God, when he declares that "the message which we have heard" from Christ is this: "God is light, and in him is no darkness at all." Therefore, if we are to have fellowship with God, it is evident that we must "walk in the light." This means that we must be righteous, and must love one another and must believe in Jesus Christ.

Thus righteousness is the first test of fellowship with God. It is very obvious that the proof of being a Christian is found in the life one leads. Yet the application of this test is more difficult than may at first appear. It may result in discouragement or in self-deception. Some Christians are so conscious of sin that if righteousness is the test, they may conclude that they have no fellowship with God; others are so certain of fellowship with God, that, as righteousness is the test of such fellowship, they conclude they have no sin.

It is reassuring, then, to find that as John applies this test, first negatively and then positively, the first application centers in the consciousness of sin, as the second centers in the doing of righteousness. That is to say, if we walk in the light which God has revealed, we cannot fail to be aware of our sinfulness. The greatest saints have been most painfully conscious of their imperfection. It is true, however, that sin has not been the purpose and intent of their lives. One who refuses to accept the moral light revealed in Christ, and who is unwilling to obey that light, cannot have fellowship with God: "If we say that we have fellowship with him and walk in the darkness, we lie, and do not the truth." John mentions three such falsehoods, and three contrasted truths. To say that one is a Christian, while he is walking in darkness, is a lie; this "walking in darkness" does not mean necessarily to live in vice or immorality, but to pursue the daily task without reference to the will of God, to live according to worldly standards, to seek selfish goals, to exclude the light offered in Christ; this is to make impossible our fellowship with God.

In contrast with this falsehood, John states the unexpected truth, not that if we walk in the light we have fellowship with God, which would have been a natural conclusion to his sentence, but this related truth, that such a walk insures fellowship with other Christians, and continual cleansing from the daily sins of which we are conscious.

This first falsehood, then, consists in saying that sin is a matter of no consequence, that a man can live without regard to the will of God and still enjoy fellowship with God.

The second of these falsehoods which men are tempted to utter declares that we are not responsible for sin. "If we say that we have no sin, we deceive ourselves, and the truth is not in us." Here John protests not only against the theories of his own day which taught that evil resided in matter and is not a concern of the spirit, but also against the materialists of our own day who insist that sin is a question of body, or mind, an affection of the brain, a result of inheritance or surroundings, a consequence of education or social customs. John declares that it is caused by the human will, and that it involves man in guilt. He adds, however, that "if we confess our sins, he is faithful

and righteous to forgive us our sins, and to cleanse us
from all unrighteousness."

A third false view which a Christian is tempted to take
of himself denies that in his own case sin exists. As to this
claim of sinlessness John declares, "If we say that we have
not sinned, we make him a liar, and his word is not in us."

If sin is universal, however, there is likewise a universal
provision for sin. The writer does not mean to encourage
sin, but to comfort one who has sinned. "My little children, these things write I unto you that ye may not sin.
And if any man sin, we have an Advocate with the Father,
Jesus Christ the righteous: and he is the propitiation for
our sins; and not for ours only, but also for the whole
world." The provision is thus twofold: intercession, and
propitiation. The last word indicates a sacrifice in virtue
of which sin is "covered" and its guilt is removed. Just
before, we were told that "the blood of Jesus his Son
cleanseth us from all sin," and further that God "is faithful and righteous to forgive us our sins, and to cleanse us
from all unrighteousness." So our thought here is led to
the atoning work of Christ. By means of his death, sin is
pardoned, the barrier is removed, and fellowship with
God is restored. Christ is also our "Advocate"; this is
the beautiful word "Paraclete" or "Comforter"; it defines
one who stands near to render help, and particularly to
plead one's cause. He is certain to secure our pardon for
he is "righteous" and he pleads with the Father who loves
us and who himself "sent the Son to be the Saviour of the
world."

It is evident then that walking in the light involves a
consciousness of sin as moral guilt and as interrupting our
fellowship with God; but it also involves an experience of
pardon conditioned on our repentance and confession and
upon the death and intercession of Christ.

Yet this "walking in the light" includes not only the
recognition of what is true, but the doing of what is right.
The knowledge of God, or fellowship with God, is tested

positively by obedience to the divine commands. "And hereby we know that we know him, if we keep his commandments." No boasted acquaintance with sacred truths, no glib acceptance of a lengthy creed, are proofs of divine fellowship. "He that saith, I know him, and keepeth not his commandments, is a liar, and the truth is not in him." Real fellowship with God, in which is developed his love for us and our love for him, is proved by doing his will: "Whoso keepeth his word, in him verily hath the love of God been perfected." Even as Christ was ever delighting to do the will of his Father, so our claim of a continuing fellowship with God will be attested by our faithful following of Christ: "He that saith he abideth in him ought himself also to walk even as he walked."

b. Tested by Love Ch. 2:7-17

7 Beloved, no new commandment write I unto you, but an old commandment which ye had from the beginning: the old commandment is the word which ye heard. 8 Again, a new commandment write I unto you, which thing is true in him and in you; because the darkness is passing away, and the true light already shineth. 9 He that saith he is in the light and hateth his brother, is in the darkness even until now. 10 He that loveth his brother abideth in the light, and there is no occasion of stumbling in him. 11 But he that hateth his brother is in the darkness, and walketh in the darkness, and knoweth not whither he goeth, because the darkness hath blinded his eyes.

12 I write unto you, my little children, because your sins are forgiven you for his name's sake. 13 I write unto you, fathers, because ye know him who is from the beginning. I write unto you, young men, because ye have overcome the evil one. I have written unto you, little children, because ye know the Father. 14 I have written unto you, fathers, because ye know him who is from the beginning. I have written unto you, young men, because ye are strong, and the word of God abideth in you, and ye have overcome the evil one. 15 Love not the world, neither the things that are in the world. If any man love the world,

the love of the Father is not in him. 16 For all that is in the world, the lust of the flesh and the lust of the eyes and the vainglory of life, is not of the Father, but is of the world. 17 And the world passeth away, and the lust thereof: but he that doeth the will of God abideth for ever.

One who is walking in the light revealed by Christ will not only do what is right in refraining from sin, he will also keep the great commandment of love which Christ gave and himself fulfilled. Love is an inevitable test of fellowship with God. In applying the test of righteousness, the writer showed that it is manifested negatively in the consciousness and confession of sin, and positively in the perception and performance of duty. So in dealing with this second test, he shows that it consists, positively, in loving one's brother (vs. 7-11) and, negatively, in not loving the world (vs. 12-17).

In introducing this test, John does not name it; he does, however, use a new term to describe his readers; he calls them "Beloved," and thus expresses love when about to encourage love. He designates his subject by calling it the "commandment" which is at once "old" and "new." Since their first acquaintance with Christ, his followers had known that the great law of life was love. Even Moses, centuries before, had set forth love as embodying and comprehending all law. Christ, however, had given to love a new standard and a new motive. His followers were to love one another as he had loved them, and for his sake. In them and in him love was finding its real expression; as John writes, "which thing is true in him and in you." He is the more eager to remind his readers of this commandment, because the light which the gospel reveals, the light of God's real nature, is dispelling the darkness of moral ignorance; and as the chief excellence of that light is love, the followers of Christ should assure themselves that they are walking in the light by keeping the "old" commandment which has become "new."

This test is not difficult to apply: "He that saith he is in the light and hateth his brother, is in darkness even until now." Even though one boasts his spiritual enlightenment, even though the "true light" may be shining all about him, if he hates his brother he is really walking in darkness. "He that loveth his brother abideth in the light, and there is no occasion of stumbling in him," that is, there is nothing in his heart and disposition which may occasion him to stumble and fall, no anger or pride or envy or thirst for revenge. These perils one avoids who walks in the light of love. On the other hand "he that hateth his brother is in the darkness, and walketh in the darkness, and knoweth not whither he goeth, because the darkness hath blinded his eyes." Surely nothing is so blind as hatred; it conceals from us our faults, and the virtues of others. It keeps us in ignorance of our moral peril and indifferent to the consequences of our deeds. No one who lives under the power of hatred, no one who fails to obey the impulse of love, can claim fellowship with God, for "God is love."

Before turning to the negative application of this text, to explain why he speaks so earnestly, or to prepare the way for his solemn warning against the love of the world, John makes a sixfold statement of the spiritual character and attainments of those to whom he is writing. He says in effect that the reason for his message is not any doubt as to their Christian standing or progress, but rather to encourage them to further achievements and to caution them against temptations from which even they cannot be free. This statement brings to modern readers of this epistle the reminder that we are urged to do righteousness and to manifest love, not that we may become Christians, but because we already enjoy fellowship with God, and are seeking for a larger realization of all the privileges such fellowship allows; and further, it suggests that even such persons as are here described are not beyond the reach of the perilous allurements and fascinations of the world.

The reasons combined in this sixfold statement are arranged in two parallel series of three each. The first in each series is addressed to the readers in general, the second to the more mature readers, and the third to the younger among them. "Little children" is the term which the writer applies to all his readers, to whom he stands in the affectionate relation of a spiritual father. He declares that he is writing to them "because your sins are forgiven you for his name's sake." It is easy to see why this stands first. The forgiveness of sins is the initial and fundamental experience of a Christian; it is the supreme need of every soul; it is the absolute condition of fellowship with God, and the main message of the epistle has been concerned with the provision for this pardon in the "blood," the "cleansing," the advocacy, the "propitiation," of Jesus Christ.

The second reason for addressing all his readers is this: "because ye know the Father." This knowledge is made possible through Christ; it is the very essence of "eternal life"; it is capable of continual development, but, like the forgiveness of sins, it is an experience common to all Christians.

When John turns to address the more mature among his readers, he calls them "fathers," and in each instance the reason assigned is this: "because ye know him who is from the beginning." The reference is to Christ, and the suggestion is that through him comes the knowledge of God, and that this knowledge increases in its depth and fullness by the experiences of life, by the pressure of problems, by the stress of sorrows, by the changes and mysteries of the passing years.

The other special group of readers whom John addresses are the "young men." He declares that he writes to them with the full consciousness that they "are strong," that "the word of God abideth" in them, and that they "have overcome the evil one." It is for this very reason that he can summon them to further conflict in the battle against "the world" and all its enticements. For such a struggle they are prepared; they have been given divine strength, the word of God is their weapon, and they are confident in the victories already won against the deadly enemy of their souls.

To readers such as these, John may well give his great exhortation. Those who "know the Father" are ready to heed the warning, "Love not the world"; those who know the eternal, changeless Christ are prepared to resist the alluring seductions of time which so soon are passing away; those who have overcome the evil one are ready to withstand his familiar forms of attack in "the lust of the flesh and the lust of the eyes and the vainglory of life."

When the writer speaks here of "the world," he, of course, does not refer to the beautiful world of nature, with its changing seasons, its sunlight and flowers, its mountains, seas, and summer skies. Nor does he refer to the complex world of human relationships, with its duties and joys, its friendships, its struggles, its triumphs, and its tears. He refers to "the world" of unbelieving men and women, to the society of the unspiritual and the godless. This is "the world" we are not to love. We are not to court its favors, not to follow its customs, not to adopt its maxims, not to covet its prizes. "If any man love the world, the love of the Father is not in him." The Christless world has always been opposed to the will of God. It would be impossible for the heart to be set upon "the world," and at the same time to be filled with love for the Father. For what are the three main elements of worldly life? First, "the lust of the flesh," by which is meant not the natural appetites of the body which are innocent, but unlawful desires which seek to enslave the soul. Secondly, there is the "lust of the eyes," the appeal which is made to the aesthetic sense, to the mind, to the imagination, when this appeal is divorced from all thought of God and from all obedience to Christ. Even the love of beauty and the love of knowledge may prove to be worldly substitutes for the love of God.

Lastly, there is "the vainglory of life," the pride of place and possessions, the foolish sense of security and satisfaction in things which are so soon to vanish, the senseless gratification in conscious superiority to others; surely these are "not of the Father," but they form the familiar features of "the world."

On many grounds it would be easy to condemn the "love of the world" which excludes the "love of the Father"; John mentions but one, and solemnly declares the wisdom of a contrary choice: "And the world passeth away, and the lust thereof: but he that doeth the will of God abideth for ever."

c. Tested by Belief   Ch. 2:18-29

18 Little children, it is the last hour: and as ye heard that antichrist cometh, even now have there arisen many antichrists; whereby we know that it is the last hour. 19 They went out from us, but they were not of us; for if they had been of us, they would have continued with us: but they went out, *that they might be made manifest that they all are not of us. 20 And ye have an anointing from the Holy One, and ye know all things. 21 I have not written unto you because ye know not the truth, but because ye know it, and because no lie is of the truth. 22 Who is the liar but he that denieth that Jesus is the Christ? This is the antichrist,* even *he that denieth the Father and the Son. 23 Whosoever denieth the Son, the same hath not the Father: he that confesseth the Son hath the Father also. 24 As for you, let that abide in you which ye heard from the beginning. If that which ye heard from the beginning abide in you, ye also shall abide in the Son, and in the Father. 25 And this is the promise which he promised us,* even *the life eternal. 26 These things have I written unto you concerning them that would lead you astray. 27 And as for you, the anointing which ye received of him abideth in you, and ye need not that any one teach you; but as his anointing teacheth you concerning all things, and is true,*

and is no lie, and even as it taught you, ye abide in him.
28 And now, my *little children, abide in him; that, if he*
shall be manifested, we may have boldness, and not be
ashamed before him at his coming. 29 If ye know that
he is righteous, ye know that every one also that doeth
righteousness is begotten of him.

John had just been speaking of the passing away of
"the world." He referred to the close of this present age,
to the coming of Christ, and the consequent end of that
order in which lust and selfishness and vanity are controlling principles. Now he affirms that the time may be
near: "Little children, it is the last hour." The proof is
found in the present unbelief and opposition to Christ.
It has been predicted that when Christ returns there will
be in existence a "man of sin," "the beast," the "antichrist," whom the Lord will destroy. The manifestation
of this antichristian spirit is a sure sign that his coming
may not be far distant: "Ye heard that antichrist cometh,
even now have there arisen many antichrists; whereby we
know that it is the last hour." These "antichrists" John
sees in the persons of the false teachers who have with-
drawn from the church. Their withdrawal is a sure proof
that they never shared in the real life and fellowship of the
Christian communion; otherwise they never would have
fallen away: "They went out from us, but they were not
of us; for if they had been of us, they would have continued with us." Their going out, however, is providential,
and is a real benefit to the church: "They went out, that
they might be made manifest that they all are not of us."
The peril to the church was much greater before the
fact was thus manifested that none of these false teachers
was a real Christian.

John insists, however, that even had these false profes-
sors remained in the church, his readers would have de-
tected them; for the Holy Spirit abiding with all believers
gives to them sure knowledge of the vital truths which
these apostate teachers deny. This is what is meant by the

statement: "And ye have an anointing from the Holy One, and we know all things." The Spirit enables one to distinguish essential truth from error; and surely these have nothing in common "because no lie is of the truth."

The special error against which the readers are warned relates to the person of Christ: "Who is the liar but he that denieth that Jesus is the Christ?" By the term "Christ" is meant not merely the "Messiah" as predicted by the Hebrew prophets, but the "Son of God," the eternal "Word" of whom John writes. To deny the "incarnation," to deny that the "Word" who "was God," "became flesh," to deny that Jesus is at once the ideal Man and the true God, is the supreme lie: "This is the antichrist." The last word denotes one who is opposed to Christ and also one who appears under the guise of Christ. It intimates the pernicious and delusive influence of those who profess the name of Christian and yet deny that Jesus is the "Son of God." Such a denial is said to involve a denial of the Father and the Son, for if Jesus Christ was not God "manifested in the flesh," as he claimed to be, then we have no full and saving revelation of God: "Whosoever denieth the Son, the same hath not the Father: he that confesseth the Son hath the Father also."

In view of the prevalence of such false teaching, the readers are urged to keep in their hearts, continually, the truth concerning Christ which they have received from his inspired apostles; for if that abides in them, such a knowledge of God in Christ will result in fellowship with God, or as John here affirms, in "the life eternal."

Thus solemn is the warning against the seductions of false teachers. The preceding paragraph was a warning against the allurements of "the world." There love of the world was declared to be a proof that one did not love God, and so was not in fellowship with God; here, denial of the truth concerning Christ is declared to indicate this lack of divine fellowship. Belief is thus shown to be a touchstone of character; it is a test of life. It is more than

an intellectual assent to truth; it has its moral elements
as well; it consists in submission to a Being who is holy
and divine. It is a spiritual experience made abiding
by the indwelling Spirit of God. Therefore John again
reminds his readers of that "anointing" which they have
received, as a result of which they need not be troubled
by false teaching. "Ye need not that any one teach you,"
does not mean, however, that the readers have no need of
Christian instruction, as the former statement, "ye know
all things," does not mean that they are infallible. It does
mean that those who will ponder the gospel message, and
allow the Holy Spirit to guide them, will come to an
enlarging knowledge and a joyful assurance of the truth
concerning Christ as the divine Son of God. Thus John
closes the paragraph with the exhortation to "abide in
him; that, if he shall be manifested, we may have boldness, and not be ashamed before him at his coming."
This abiding in Christ will be by faith, but also by obedience. These are inseparable. Faith in Christ is a test of
fellowship with God, but so, too, are holiness and love.
Therefore John can add, "Ye know that every one also
that doeth righteousness is begotten of him." The best
way to assure our hearts, so that with joyful confidence we
may expect the return of Christ, is to abide in him with
loving trust and to do continually his holy will.

III
THE LIFE OF THE
CHILDREN OF GOD

Chs. 3:1 to 4:6

a. Tested by Righteousness   Ch. 3:1-10

1 Behold what manner of love the Father hath bestowed upon us, that we should be called children of God; and such we are. For this cause the world knoweth us not, because it knew him not. 2 Beloved, now are we children of God, and it is not yet made manifest what we shall be. We know that, if he shall be manifested, we shall be like him; for we shall see him even as he is. 3 And every one that hath this hope set on him purifieth himself, even as he is pure. 4 Every one that doeth sin doeth also lawlessness; and sin is lawlessness. 5 And ye know that he was manifested to take away sins; and in him is no sin. 6 Whosoever abideth in him sinneth not: whosoever sinneth hath not seen him, neither knoweth him. 7 My little children, let no man lead you astray: he that doeth righteousness is righteous, even as he is righteous: 8 he that doeth sin is of the devil; for the devil sinneth from the beginning. To this end was the Son of God manifested, that he might destroy the works of the devil. 9 Whosoever is begotten of God doeth no sin, because his seed abideth in him: and he cannot sin, because he is begotten of God. 10 In this the children of God are manifest, and the children of the devil: whosoever doeth not righteousness is not of God, neither he that loveth not his brother.

In the preceding chapters, the Christian life has been presented under the figure of a divine fellowship; in the chapter which now opens it is represented as the result of a divine birth. Believers not only enjoy fellowship with

God, they are born of God or "begotten of him"; they partake of his nature and are the "children of God." This truth was stated in the closing verse of the last chapter; in fact, that verse might well be regarded as forming the introduction to this paragraph: "If ye know that he is righteous, ye know that every one also that doeth righteousness is begotten of him." Here is affirmed both the fact that God imparts a new life, and also that the first test of this life is righteousness.

The fact is in itself surprising, astonishing; the apostle cannot repress an exclamation of wonder: "Behold what manner of love the Father hath bestowed upon us, that we should be called children of God." It should be noted that the phrase "children of God" is distinct from "sons of God." Paul more commonly employs the latter, John the former. The word "sons" denotes position, rank, legal relationship; but "children" denotes birth, origin, oneness of nature; it is like the Scotch term "bairns"; it means "born ones." The thought here is not of "sonship," as is commonly stated, but of a new birth; not of "adoption" but of "regeneration." In the infinite love of God, he grants to all who believe in Christ a change of moral nature, a new disposition, a spiritual experience, so vital that he does not hesitate to call them his "children," to acknowledge them as such, and to regard and treat them as such: "As many as received him, to them gave he the right to become children of God, even to them that believe on his name: who were born, not of blood, nor of the will of the flesh, nor the will of man, but of God."

However surprising these statements may seem, however great the mysteries involved, the reality is beyond question; so that John adds emphatically, "and such we are." The words do not apply to all men. "We, Christians, are called children of God," is what John is saying. While it is true that God is the Father of all men, and they are all his children, by creation, yet it is also true that there is a "new creation," and that those who believe in Christ are children of a heavenly birth, are truly born of God, are the real "children of God." The true Fatherhood of God is never fully appreciated until one draws near to him through Christ, and the brotherhood of man will never be realized until men find the Father through Jesus Christ his Son.

Instead of including all men in the term "children of God," John by that term sharply distinguishes Christians from the whole mass of unbelieving men and women; "for this cause the world knoweth us not, because it knew him not." Those who reject Christ should not be expected to understand the followers of Christ. The world "knew him not," even "his own [countrymen] received him not"; it is not strange then that the world has no sympathy with the motives and aims and character of the "children of God" who follow in his steps or reproduce his life. True Christians will ever be mysterious to unbelievers. The difference, moreover, is destined to become greater. Christians, as the children of God, are growing in likeness to the Son of God; and "we know that, if he shall be manifested, we shall be like him; for we shall see him even as he is." This blessed hope, to be realized at the coming of Christ, concerns chiefly the character, the disposition, the moral nature which will be transformed and made perfect, by the direct and glorious vision of the Lord; yet it includes the transfiguration of the body, which is to be "conformed to the body of his glory."

All these experiences and privileges belong to those whom God calls his children; but who are they? how can they be discerned? how will their nature be manifested? John replies: "And every one that hath this hope set on him purifieth himself, even as he is pure." It is only natural to suppose that one whose life is fixed upon Christ will be imitating Christ, and particularly in the matter of avoiding sin and of doing righteousness. John enforces this idea by three or four considerations: first, by the nature of sin; it is "lawlessness," and one who is a child of God surely will not disregard and defy the law of God; secondly, by the nature of Christ and of his work: "He was manifested to take away sins; and in him is no sin"; evidently then a man who sins can have no real acquaintance with Christ: he "hath not seen him, neither knoweth him"; thirdly, by the fact that "sin is of the devil"; by their attitude toward sin, then, "the children of God are manifest, and the children of the devil"; fourthly, by the character of the "new birth"; it consists in the imparting of a new life principle, a divine germ; out of it sin could not possibly develop: "Whosoever is begotten of God doeth no sin, because his seed abideth in him: and he cannot sin, because he is begotten of God."

From all this, it is easy to understand that if a man is a Christian he will do what is right; if we are "children of God" we may be expected to resemble him in righteousness. A grave difficulty, however, exists in the absolute and unqualified terms which John employs. He says that a Christian "doeth no sin," and even "cannot sin." As a matter of fact we know that Christians do sin; and John, in the first two and in the last chapters of his epistle, tells us that Christians can sin and suggests what they are to do to find pardon and cleansing when they have sinned.

The difficulty is resolved by some in supposing that the reference is to a particular class of Christians who attain sinless perfection; but this contradicts the simple statement of the apostle which is universal: "Whosoever is begotten of God doeth no sin . . . and he cannot sin."

Others suppose the reference is to the ideal and theoretical experience of a Christian; he is a man who does not expect to sin, and is not supposed to sin, although practically he does sin at times. However, the words of John are rather too definite for such an explanation; they refer to actual sin; and they say that one "begotten of God . . . cannot sin."

Others explain that the "new nature" cannot sin, though the "old nature" may; this involves a false theory of the human mind; such belief in a dual personality or a divided self finds no support in Scripture or in science.

Still others suppose that the reference is to habitual states, or regular practice; that, John means to say, simply, that a Christian will not usually, or continually, sin. However, the language is too definite for this possible explanation; the statement is, he "cannot sin."

It may possibly be best to find the explanation in view of the errors John is attempting to combat. He has false teachers in mind. "My little children, let no man lead you astray: he that doeth righteousness is righteous." Evidently these teachers were suggesting that a man might be righteous even though he were doing what is wrong. There were those who claimed that sin concerned only the body, and that, in spite of impurity of life, the soul might not be stained; and others taught that sinful acts might not interfere with high spiritual states. John is therefore making an unqualified denial of an unmitigated lie. In other parts of the epistle he makes plain his understanding that all Christians do sin and have need of continual cleansing. Here, however, he is sharply rebuking those who would make light of sin, or disguise its satanic character. He does not pause to make any deductions or obvious qualifications. He declares the absolute opposition between sin and holiness, between lawlessness and righteousness, between the "children of the devil" and the "children of God." Whatever difficulty may be involved in his particular words, he burns into our souls the truth that one who has his hope set on Christ will purify himself "even as he is pure."

b. Tested by Love   Ch. 3:11-24

11 For this is the message which ye heard from the beginning, that we should love one another: 12 not as Cain was of the evil one, and slew his brother. And wherefore slew he him? Because his works were evil, and his brother's righteous.

13 Marvel not, brethren, if the world hateth you. 14 We know that we have passed out of death into life, be-

*cause we love the brethren. He that loveth not abideth in
death. 15 Whosoever hateth his brother is a murderer: and
ye know that no murderer hath eternal life abiding in him.
16 Hereby know we love, because he laid down his life for
us: and we ought to lay down our lives for the brethren.
17 But whoso hath the world's goods, and beholdeth his
brother in need, and shutteth up his compassion from him,
how doth the love of God abide in him? 18 My little children, let us not love in word, neither with the tongue; but
in deed and truth. 19 Hereby shall we know that we are
of the truth, and shall assure our heart before him: 20
because if our heart condemn us, God is greater than our
heart, and knoweth all things. 21 Beloved, if our heart
condemn us not, we have boldness toward God; 22 and
whatsoever we ask we receive of him, because we keep his
commandments and do the things that are pleasing in his
sight. 23 And this is his commandment, that we should
believe in the name of his Son Jesus Christ, and love one
another, even as he gave us commandment. 24 And he
that keepeth his commandments abideth in him, and he in
him. And hereby we know that he abideth in us, by the
Spirit which he gave us.*

The link between this section and that which precedes
is found in the tenth verse of the chapter: "In this the
children of God are manifest, and the children of the devil:
whosoever doeth not righteousness is not of God, neither
he that loveth nor his brother." The previous paragraph
applied to the Christian life the test of righteousness; here
is applied the test of love. The writer regards it as an
obvious test, for he declares that the whole message of the
life and character of Christ was a message of love. From
the beginning of their acquaintance with him it had been
known by his followers that they must obey his law of
love: "For this is the message which ye heard from the
beginning, that we should love one another." One who
is a child of God will surely obey the law revealed by the
Son of God.

To impress the validity of this test, the writer is about

to dwell upon the supreme example of self-sacrifice given by Christ; but he first summons to our memory the darkly contrasting figure of Cain. The demonic nature of this first murderer is evinced by the motive which inspired his cruel deed; it was envy, one of the most subtle and common and deadly forms of hatred: "Cain was of the evil one, and slew his brother. . . . Because his works were evil, and his brother's righteous." Therefore Christians, who by their righteousness show themselves children of God, need not be surprised at the enmity of the unbelieving world: "Marvel not, brethren, if the world hateth you." Hatred is so natural and so universal, that love is a certain proof of the presence in one of a new life principle, of the experience of a new birth, of the possession of a new moral nature: "We know that we have passed out of death into life, because we love the brethren." If one is not animated by love, then evidently he is still in a state of spiritual death, he has not been born of God, he is not a "child of God." "He that loveth not abideth in death." As Christ himself taught, in his Sermon on the Mount, whosoever hates his brother is a murderer, for he is cherishing the motive which would result in the act, were all restraints removed and were opportunity given. Surely one who is so disposed cannot have the nature of God, cannot be a "child of God," cannot have "eternal life": "Ye know that no murderer hath eternal life abiding in him."

In contrast with Cain, the embodiment of hatred, stands the radiant form of Christ, the revelation of love: "Hereby know we love, because he laid down his life for us." His death "for us" is not only the supreme proof of his love; it is the required measurement of ours: "and we ought to lay down our lives for the brethren." When occasion arises, when necessity demands, we ought to show such devotion; we owe it to others, we owe it to Christ, we owe it to ourselves, for thus we show ourselves to be the children of God. These present years are giving countless examples of such heroic self-sacrifice; but tests of a less dramatic character are ever at hand: "Whoso hath the world's goods, and beholdeth his brother in need, and shutteth up his compassion from him, how doth the love of God abide in him?" This "love of God" is the love which is of the nature of God; it is a manifestation of that new life which God gives to his children. Lacking this "love of God," how can one claim to be a child of God? Let love be shown then, if we are Christians, not by our hymns and our professions alone, nor by our admiration of high motives and heroic acts, but by our daily lives: "My little children, let us not love in word, neither with the tongue; but in deed and truth."

It is true that when we judge ourselves by these high standards, when we apply to ourselves the "tests" insisted upon in this epistle, we are often discouraged and our hearts condemn us. Nevertheless, if love has been the guiding principle of our lives, then, in spite of occasional failures and of conscious faults, we shall have confidence that we are the children of God, that our new birth is a reality, that "we are of the truth." Even when our hearts condemn us as we are confronted with the memory of some great defeat, we will believe that "God is greater than our heart," that he "knoweth all things," and that he recognizes our love toward him, and our faith in Christ, and the reality of the new life he has implanted. Otherwise we could have no confidence in prayer; but when assured, by the test of love, that we are the children of God, then we speak to him with freedom, as to a loving Father, and then "whatsoever we ask we receive of him, because we keep his commandments." This latter does not mean that our prayers are answered as a reward of merit, but rather that keeping his commandments shows that we are at one with his will, and so living and praying as he would have us, our petitions are certain to be fulfilled.

Speaking of "commandments," John reminds us that they are all largely comprehended in the requirements to believe in Christ, and to love one another. The first of these requirements he emphasizes in the following paragraph; the second has been his theme in this, and he only pauses to insist that keeping these commandments is both a condition and a result of true fellowship with God; it deepens the assurance which is imparted to us by the Spirit of God, for "hereby we know that he abideth in us, by the Spirit which he gave us."

c. Tested by Belief   Ch. 4:1-6

1 Beloved, believe not every spirit, but prove the spirits, whether they are of God; because many false prophets are gone out into the world. 2 Hereby know ye the Spirit of God: every spirit that confesseth that Jesus Christ is come in the flesh is of God: 3 and every spirit that confesseth not Jesus is not of God: and this is the spirit of the antichrist, whereof ye have heard that it cometh; and now it is in the world already. 4 Ye are of God, my little children, and have overcome them: because greater is he that is in you than he that is in the world. 5 They are of the world: therefore speak they as of the world, and the world heareth them. 6 We are of God: he that knoweth God heareth us; he who is not of God heareth us not. By this we know the spirit of truth, and the spirit of error.

It is noticeable that in this epistle the work of the Holy Spirit, or to use the title employed by John, the work of "the Spirit," or the work of "the Spirit of God," is related almost exclusively to the imparting of faith and the inspiring of belief. Of course he has other functions; but John refers to him as specifically "the spirit of truth," whom Jesus thus described, and of whom he said, "He shall guide you into all the truth" and "He shall bear witness of me."

Therefore, as in the close of the last chapter, belief "in the name of his Son Jesus Christ" is related to the presence of "the Spirit which he gave us," so, as this chapter opens, the assurance that one is a child of God is based on the confession, inspired by the Spirit of God, that "Jesus Christ is come in the flesh."

There are manifest among men many other "spirits," and many false teachers, who claim to be inspired of God; against these John warns his readers and declares that the crucial test of all teachers is their attitude toward Christ: "Beloved, believe not every spirit, but prove the spirits, whether they are of God; . . . every spirit that confesseth not Jesus is not of God." Those to whom John referred had "gone out into the world"; they had left the church and joined the society of the godless and the unbelieving; they claimed to be "spiritual," to be "Christian," to be "divinely inspired," but in reality their "spirit" was that of antichrist; even worse, it was the "spirit" of the "prince of this world," the devil. By these "false prophets," however, the readers of the epistle had not been led astray; as the children of God, they had been strengthened by the Spirit of God and had defeated "the spirit of error"; "Ye are of God," writes the apostle, "and have overcome them: because greater is he that is in you than he that is in the world." These "false prophets," nevertheless, were very popular; they were "of the world," their spirit was in perfect sympathy with the spirit of the world, and as their teachings were determined by this spirit, they were consequently exactly such as the world delighted to hear. By way of contrast, John and his fellow apostles claimed to be "of God," and to be guided by his Spirit; therefore the children of God received their testimony, which the "false prophets" and the world rejected: "We are of God: he that knoweth God heareth us; he who is not of God heareth us not." From all that has gone before, the apostle concludes that it is always possible to distinguish between truth and error; by the attitude toward Christ, as truly human while very God, every spirit can be tested, whether the spirit is that of a "false prophet," or of an apostle, or of the humblest and most obscure believer: "Every spirit that confesseth that Jesus Christ is come in the flesh is of

God: . . . By this we know the spirit of truth, and the spirit of error."

As in the days of John, so today many false prophets have "gone out into the world." Never have there existed a larger number of conflicting voices claiming to teach not only religions but Christian truth. We need to test the spirits. We must remember that "spiritual" does not necessarily mean "holy"; many teachers who claim to deal with mysteries and "visions" in realms which are beyond the visible and the material, many, too, who proclaim lofty sentiments and poetic fancies, are themselves false and ignorant and impure.

Nor yet does "supernatural" mean "divine." What John actually meant by the word "spirits" may be a matter of dispute; he surely implied that beings of a superhuman order are not therefore "of God," but may be satanic and demonic. We live at a time when, as never before, men are seeking aid from "spirits." Broken and bleeding hearts groping in the dark for comfort, longing for messages from loved ones whom death has snatched away, are turning in pitiful credulity to those who claim communion with the unseen world. That the "mediums" through whom these "messages" come, are usually fraudulent and deceitful, it is not difficult to prove. Even admitting some modicum of reality in their claims does not forbid the conclusion that the source of their alleged power is demonic. The real test which must be applied is this: "Every spirit that confesseth not Jesus is not of God." Confronted by some things which are mysterious, threatened by countless delusions which hide under the name of "Christian," opposed by systems of proud unbelief, we do well today to heed the warning of the apostle: "Beloved, believe not every spirit, but prove the spirits, whether they are of God."

What strange contrasts John here sets forth: the church and the world, the spirit of truth and the spirit of error, Christ and Satan, false prophets and inspired apostles, the

Spirit of God and the spirit of antichrist; but the line of cleavage is clearly stated: there is one invariable test—the attitude toward Jesus, the divine Son of God. Above all the problems in the world of religion and philosophy, there stands forth one supreme question: "What think ye of Christ?" This furnishes the touchstone of character, the test of belief, the proof of spiritual life.

IV
THE SOURCE OF LOVE
Ch. 4:7-21

7 Beloved, let us love one another: for love is of God; and every one that loveth is begotten of God, and knoweth God. 8 He that loveth not knoweth not God; for God is love. 9 Herein was the love of God manifested in us, that God hath sent his only begotten Son into the world that we might live through him. 10 Herein is love, not that we loved God, but that he loved us, and sent his Son to be the propitiation for our sins. 11 Beloved, if God so loved us, we also ought to love one another. 12 No man hath beheld God at any time: if we love one another, God abideth in us, and his love is perfected in us: 13 hereby we know that we abide in him and he in us, because he hath given us of his Spirit. 14 And we have beheld and bear witness that the Father hath sent the Son to be the Saviour of the world. 15 Whosoever shall confess that Jesus is the Son of God, God abideth in him, and he in God. 16 And we know and have believed the love which God hath in us. God is love; and he that abideth in love abideth in God, and God abideth in him. 17 Herein is love made perfect with us, that we may have boldness in the day of judgment; because as he is, even so are we in this world. 18 There is no fear in love: but perfect love casteth out fear, because fear hath punishment; and he that feareth is not made perfect in love. 19 We love, because he first loved us. 20 If a man say, I love God, and hateth his brother, he is a liar: for he that loveth not his brother whom he hath seen, cannot love God whom he hath not seen. 21 And this commandment have we from him, that he who loveth God love his brother also.

Twice before in the course of this epistle love has been treated as a test of Christian life. In the second chapter it was the "commandment" which one in fellowship with God would keep; in the third, it was a sign of likeness to the Father, which "children of God" would show; here it is a disposition which is traced to its source in the very nature of God as manifested in the gift of his Son. In following this thought, the writer reaches the profoundest depths and loftiest heights of his discussion. The paragraph is a worthy complement to the matchless "hymn of love" sung by Paul in the thirteenth chapter of his Epistle to the Corinthians, for it gives to the virtue which Paul praises its mighty motive, and finds its birth in the being of God.

From another point of view also, the epistle here reaches a climax and is found to be no mere series of tests by which a fact is discovered or on which an assurance is to be based, but a practical message of encouragement. It is designed not only to give tests of life, but to urge the fuller manifestations of that life. It is intended to secure not a mental verdict but a moral resolve, not a surer belief but a deeper experience. "Beloved," writes the apostle, "let us love one another."

The exhortation is enforced by the statement that "love is of God"; it is therefore the supreme test both of being born of God and of having fellowship with God: "Every one that loveth is begotten of God, and knoweth God. He that loveth not knoweth not God; for God is love." This sublime statement as to the nature of God is unsurpassed in all Scripture: "God is love." Twice in this brief paragraph the truth is affirmed. Here the statement is followed by a description of the supreme expression of divine love: "Herein was the love of God manifested in us, that God hath sent his only begotten Son into the world that we might live through him." This is in fact the expression of love in its very essence: "Herein is love, not that we loved God, but that he loved us, and sent his Son to be the propitiation for our sins." Thus the love of God was shown in the greatness of his gift: he not only sent a

Savior; he sent his own Son, his only Son. His love appeared further in the benefit received, namely, life, eternal life, for all believers: "that we might live through him." This was ideal, essential love, for it was shown toward the unworthy and unlovely. The love of man for God would not have been so surprising, but, "Herein is love, not that we loved God, but that he loved us." This love involved an infinite cost of sacrifice, of suffering, and of death, to secure the forgiveness of sins; this God provided; he "sent his Son to be the propitiation for our sins."

If such is the nature of God's love, we must show that we are his children by a love like his, in its disposition toward others, and in a love which finds its supreme motive in gratitude for the gift of his Son. First then, in passion for the good of others, our life must be manifested: "Beloved, if God so loved us, we also ought to love one another." It is our duty, but it is the necessary expression of our nature, not only to love God for his goodness, but "to love one another," for God is invisible; we can seek or desire to confer no benefit on him: "No man hath beheld God at any time"; but if we seek the good of others, then we manifest his nature: "God abideth in us, and his love is perfected in us." We are certain that he dwells within, for love is the fruit of his Spirit; "hereby we know that we abide in him and he in us, because he hath given us of his Spirit." More particularly, his Spirit is the Author of belief; and our love has a divine source if it is associated with the acceptance of Christ as our divine and crucified Savior, and if this belief becomes the motive of our love for one another: "We have beheld and bear witness that the Father hath sent the Son to be the Saviour of the world. Whosoever shall confess that Jesus is the Son of God, God abideth in him, and he in God." In him we see the love of God manifested: "And we know and have believed the love which God hath in us. God is love; and he that abideth in love abideth in God, and God abideth in him."

God is love, but love is not God. Not every manifestation of charity or kindness or benevolence or sacrifice is a sign of a new birth or of being a child of God. We must take our stand near the cross. When love is associated with faith and devotion toward Jesus the Son of God, then it becomes a proof of "life eternal."

From such love two results are certain to follow: confidence toward God, and charity toward men. If we fully realize the love of God revealed in Christ, we shall not stand in dread of God; and if this love is the principle of our lives we shall have no fear of judgment, for, as the children of God, we are in this world like Christ the Son of God, in our love, our confidence, our trustful relation to the Father: "Herein is love made perfect with us, that we may have boldness in the day of judgment; because as he is, even so are we in this world. There is no fear in love: but perfect love casteth out fear, because fear hath punishment; and he that feareth is not made perfect in love."

Quite as truly, if we realize God's love for us, we shall love one another: "We love, because he first loved us." Not only do we love God, but love becomes the animating principle of our life. This principle has its source in the love of God for us. It finds its natural and first expression in our love for one another. "If a man say, I love God, and hateth his brother, he is a liar: for he that loveth not his brother whom he hath seen, cannot love God whom he hath not seen." The test is simple and obvious. If one does not love his brother, then love is not ruling his life. It is foolish to boast of love, particularly to an unseen person, when love is not being shown and felt toward one who is seen daily, walking in the same sphere of life, to whom it is much more easy to express affection and devotion. Life cannot have two supreme motives, two opposing ruling principles. Love for God is inseparable from love for men. Hatred for men is a proof that love is not controlling the life; it shows one to be a liar if he is boast-

ing his love for God.   Christ himself taught us that if one
is keeping the supreme commandment he will love God
with his whole heart and his neighbor as himself: "This
commandment have we from him, that he who loveth God
love his brother also."

V

THE TRIUMPH
OF RIGHTEOUSNESS

Ch. 5:1-5

1 Whosoever believeth that Jesus is the Christ is begotten of God: and whosoever loveth him that begat loveth him also that is begotten of him. 2 Hereby we know that we love the children of God, when we love God and do his commandments. 3 For this is the love of God, that we keep his commandments: and his commandments are not grievous. 4 For whatsoever is begotten of God overcometh the world: and this is the victory that hath overcome the world, even *our faith. 5 And who is he that overcometh the world, but he that believeth that Jesus is the Son of God?*

In these brief, beautiful phrases we are facing the great, molding thoughts of the epistle. Here the life imparted by God to his children is tested by righteousness, by love, and by belief. Here, also, appears the close relation between these three elements of the Christian life; love is shown by righteousness, and righteousness is secured by faith. Here, as in no previous paragraph, the way of keeping God's commandments, the way of overcoming the world, is pointed out; here we are shown how righteousness may triumph over sin.

We should notice, however, what is said of belief and of love. The former is mentioned as an absolute proof that one is a child of God: "Whosoever believeth that Jesus is the Christ is begotten of God." Here the term "Christ" refers not only to the redeeming work of Jesus, or to his "anointing" by the Spirit of God for that work, but, more specifically, to his divine nature; it has its parallel in the last phrase of the fifth verse: "Jesus is the Son of God." One who does not so believe is not a child of God, and has no right to the name of Christian; for to deny this truth is to manifest the Spirit of antichrist. However, it is of comfort and cheer to the humblest Christian to be assured that a real, intelligent belief in Christ as the Son of God is a positive proof of being a child of God.

As to love, John here suggests that it is also a natural expression of the new life imparted by God; and he fixes the thought again, as in the previous chapter, upon the fact that love to God and love to man are inseparable: "Whosoever loveth him that begat loveth him also that is begotten of him." It will be but natural for the child of God to love the children of God; this is but the instinct of the new birth. John adds, however, what is of vital importance, and what until now he has not stated with such clearness, namely, that love to man must be regulated and characterized by love and obedience to God: "Hereby we know that we love the children of God, when we love God and do his commandments." That is, we know that our love is of the right kind, we know that it is truly love, we know that the sentiment is worthy of the name, when it is in accord with love to God and submission to his will. There is much that is called by the name of love which is purely selfish, even sinful. It is well for us to be reminded that love must be tested by righteousness. As John had previously stated that love to God is inseparable from love to men, so here he is insisting that love to men is inseparable from love to God, and that love to God is expressed in doing his will: "For this is the love of God, that we keep his commandments."

Thus John reaches the heart of this paragraph, as he mentions the "commandments" of God. He has spoken of belief and of love; he now treats of righteousness and its possible triumph. "His commandments" he affirms, "are not grievous." They are not too hard to obey; they are not unreasonable in their demands; for he gives the grace needed for their fulfillment. Of course difficulties are involved; effort is required; John does not deny this. Any man who resolves to obey God will have continual opposition. "The world" does not love God or his commandments; its maxims, its principles, its ideals, its spirit, are all contrary to his will. For the Christian, conflict is certain; but victory is likewise assured; the divine energy imparted by God is mightier than the power of the world: "For whatsoever is begotten of God overcometh the world." The weapon which secures the victory is faith. For the believer, the triumph is regarded as already won: "and this is the victory that hath overcome the world, even our faith." This is true potentially, and in principle, but practically the battle must be fought out in daily experiences. When one has put his trust in Christ he is once and for all on the side of victory; but as the unbelieving world continually assaults him, he must continually depend upon Christ for strength and for triumph. It is of interest to notice that this is the only place where the word "faith" is found, not only in this epistle but in all the writings of John. The verb "believe" is frequent. Possibly it may be the purpose of John to call attention to the object of "faith" or to the content of belief, for he at once adds: "And who is he that overcometh the world, but he that believeth that Jesus is the Son of God." It does matter what one believes relative to Jesus Christ; yet moral victory is secured not by the acceptance of certain truths about Christ, but by a definite act of faith in which the whole being is committed to him, in obedience and trust and love.

VI
THE GROUNDS OF BELIEF

6 This is he that came by water and blood, even *Jesus Christ; not with the water only, but with the water and with the blood. 7 And it is the Spirit that beareth witness, because the Spirit is the truth. 8 For there are three who bear witness, the Spirit, and the water, and the blood: and the three agree in one. 9 If we receive the witness of men, the witness of God is greater: for the witness of God is this, that he hath borne witness concerning his Son. 10 He that believeth on the Son of God hath the witness in him: he that believeth not God hath made him a liar; because he hath not believed in the witness that God hath borne concerning his Son. 11 And the witness is this, that God gave unto us eternal life, and this life is in his Son. 12 He that hath the Son hath the life; he that hath not the Son of God hath not the life.*

Having declared that victory over the world is secured by faith in Jesus as the divine Son of God, John proceeds to show the grounds on which such a belief is based. Among these he includes (*a*) historic facts, (*b*) divine testimony, (*c*) Christian experience.

a. The first proof, then, that Jesus is the Son of God is found in the gospel narrative. The works and words of Christ, together with the interpretation which he placed upon his person and mission, warrant such a belief. These facts are all summed up and symbolized in two significant events of his career, in his baptism and his crucifixion: "This is he that came by water and blood, even Jesus Christ." It will be remembered that while the body of Jesus was still hanging on the cross, after his Spirit had departed, "one of the soldiers with a spear pierced his side,

and straightway there came out blood and water." Whatever mystery may have been involved, the fact seems to
have impressed John most deeply; he alone of the Gospel
writers narrates the event and he does so in terms which
indicate his view of its signal importance. To him it was,
for whatever reason, a proof of the divine nature of his
Lord, and he records it that his readers "may believe."
So here, in his epistle, he refers to "the water" and "the
blood" as summarizing and symbolizing the whole gospel
narrative. In the water of baptism and in the blood of his
cross, Christ was manifested as the Savior of the world; he
appeared as the One who could meet the world's need of
cleansing and of pardon, of new spiritual life and of atone-
ment for sin. Then, also, at his baptism he heard the
voice of the Father saying: "This is my beloved Son"; and
at the crucifixion, when the spear was thrust into his side,
John saw the fulfillment of the prophecy which concerned
the divine Christ: "They shall look on him whom they
pierced." Thus the baptism and the crucifixion, with all
that they included and indicated, were proofs that "Jesus is
the Son of God."

John specially emphasizes the crucifixion: "Not with
the water only, but with the water and with the blood."
He was probably seeking to rebuke the heretics of his day,
who were attempting to separate between the human Jesus
and the heavenly "Christ." They held that the divine
Being, "Christ," came upon Jesus at the baptism but left
him just before his crucifixion. John affirms that the
Being who was baptized was identical with the Being who
was crucified; he was the Son of God, both in his life and
in his death. A similar error needs to be met today, as it
appears in a double aspect: first, in those who deny the
divine person of our Lord, as they attempt to distinguish
between "Jesus" and "the Christ"; and, second, in those
who deny the atoning work of our Lord, as they praise
his power to purify and ennoble life, but refuse to regard
his death as a sacrifice for sin. We need today this mes-

sage of John: "Not with the water only, but with the water
and with the blood."   First of all, then, Christian faith is
founded on historic facts.

b. The second ground of belief is found in the witness of
the Holy Spirit: "And it is the Spirit that beareth witness,
because the Spirit is the truth."   Here we may seem to be
entering the realm of mystery; but the teaching of Scripture is clear.   Christian belief is described as an inspiration of the divine Spirit.   His office is to testify to that
which is true, and particularly concerning Jesus Christ:
"The Spirit is the truth."   No one may have direct consciousness of his presence or testimony; on the other hand
no one can really believe in the divine Christ without the
aid and the illumination of the Spirit of God.   Christian
belief is not due merely to mental deductions drawn from
the facts of the gospel.   Our faith is never the ground of
boasting.   When one confesses his faith, he is reminded
that "Flesh and blood hath not revealed it unto thee, but
my Father who is in heaven."   However, the two are commonly inseparable, and they unite to establish the one
fact; the gospel narrative and the divine Spirit combine in
producing belief.   The Spirit agrees with the water and the
blood in testifying to this one great truth, that "Jesus is
the Son of God"; "For there are three who bear witness,
the Spirit, and the water, and the blood: and the three
agree in one."   The Spirit employs the word of Christ, but
also the Sacraments of the church, to inspire and sustain
our faith.   It is not strange that believers, through all the
centuries, have found references to Baptism and the Lord's
Supper in the words "the water" and "the blood."   These
ordinances the Spirit employs to set forth the cleansing and
atoning work of Christ and the new life he imparts; they
are his witnesses to the divine person and work of the
Son of God.

c. This testimony of the inspired gospel and of the divine Spirit are designated by John "the witness of God,"
and if, in human courts, concurrent testimony of accred-

ited witnesses is accepted, much more should we be convinced by such divine attestation of the Sonship of Christ:
"If we receive the witness of men, the witness of God is
greater." However, John adds a third ground of belief,
namely, Christian experience: "He that believeth on the
Son of God hath the witness in him." Faith may be regarded by some as a great venture: but one who casts himself wholly upon Christ, one who not only believes statements about him, but who believes "on" him, comes to
possess a direct and deepening consciousness that the object of his trust is none other than a divine Savior. He
has a sense of cleansing and pardon, of acceptance with
God, of peace and power and victory, and this experi-
mental knowledge of Christ confirms the belief that he is
indeed "the Son of God."

With the trust, which becomes a deepening conviction,
in the deity of Christ, John contrasts the unbelief which
rejects the testimony to his divine Sonship. Such unbelief
makes God a liar. To reject the inspired gospel, to resist
the Spirit of truth, is to accuse God of falsehood, to sus-
pect him of deceit: "He that believeth not God hath
made him a liar; because he hath not believed in the witness that God hath borne concerning his Son."

This, then, is the very sum and essence of the divine
testimony, namely, that Jesus Christ is the Son of God,
and it is, therefore, the full and perfect manifestation of
eternal life, so that, in giving us his Son, God really imparted to us this life: "And the witness is this, that God
gave unto us eternal life, and this life is in his Son." Belief in Jesus Christ as the Son of God is a proof that one
possesses this life, it is the sign that he has experienced a
new birth, it is a witness that he is a child of God: "He
that hath the Son hath the life; he that hath not the Son
of God hath not the life."

VII
CHRISTIAN CERTAINTIES

> *13 These things have I written unto you, that ye may know that ye have eternal life, even unto you that believe on the name of the Son of God. 14 And this is the boldness which we have toward him, that, if we ask anything according to his will, he heareth us: 15 and if we know that he heareth us whatsoever we ask, we know that we have the petitions which we have asked of him. 16 If any man see his brother sinning a sin not unto death, he shall ask, and God will give him life for them that sin not unto death. There is a sin unto death: not concerning this do I say that he should make request. 17 All unrighteousness is sin: and there is a sin not unto death.*
>
> *18 We know that whosoever is begotten of God sinneth not; but he that was begotten of God keepeth himself, and the evil one toucheth him not. 19 We know that we are of God, and the whole world lieth in the evil one. 20 And we know that the Son of God is come, and hath given us an understanding, that we know him that is true, and we are in him that is true, even in his Son Jesus Christ. This is the true God, and eternal life. 21 My little children, guard yourselves from idols.*

Christianity is a religion of certainties, of assured convictions, of definite beliefs. Thus, as John brings his epistle to a close, he mentions some of those realities as to which believers have confident assurance.

The first of these is the possession of eternal life: "These things have I written unto you, that ye may know that ye have eternal life, even unto you that believe on the name of the Son of God." The immediate reference is to the verses which precede; but the statement is properly taken as expressing the supreme purpose of the whole epistle. It has furnished a series of tests by which one could be assured that he possessed eternal life. The assurance is not mystical or emotional, but a rational conclusion based upon certain plain facts. These are chiefly righteousness, love, and belief. The last of these has just been emphasized, and therefore the apostle adds, "Even unto you that believe on the name of the Son of God." Those who believe are assured that, for them, "eternal life" is a present possession. This term includes the idea of future, immortal blessedness; but the element of duration is less prominent than that of moral character. "Eternal life" is the very life of God, the life manifested in Christ, and therefore, in believers, a life like that of Christ. It is given now, in its beginning, by the imparting of a new life principle; but it expands and develops until when he "shall be manifested," then, in fuller perfection, "we shall be like him; for we shall see him even as he is."

Closely related to this assurance of life is confidence in prayer: "And this is the boldness which we have toward him, that, if we ask anything according to his will, he heareth us: and if we know that he heareth us whatsoever we ask, we know that we have the petitions which we have asked of him." Prayer, therefore, is no mere empty form, it is not an impertinence, it is not irrational. It is a power whereby the will of God is brought to pass. It is humble and trustful in spirit. Its highest expression is in the words: "Not my will, but thine, be done." When the request is according to the will of God, "we have the petition" even now, for it already exists in the divine purpose and plan, and is certain to be realized in time. Whatever mysteries and perplexities may be involved in the problem of prayer, the child of God comes with boldness to make his requests known unto the Father.

One special exercise of the blessed ministry of intercession is mentioned by John: it is prayer for the spiritual restoration of a brother who has fallen into sin. But here an exception is made: a believer is not encouraged to pray with confidence for the deliverance of one who is guilty of "sin . . . unto death." The reference seems to be to those whom John has called antichrists, those who willfully and persistently deny the claims of Christ, who turn away from him and from the Christian communion, and professedly deny "the Father and the Son." The passage may be difficult, but its main purpose is plain, namely, to encourage us to fearless and sympathizing prayer for every believer who has been overtaken by a fault.

John next mentions three great verities which are included in Christian belief; they are named almost as the articles of a creed, each introduced by the confident phrase: "We know."

a. The reality, the possibility, the absolute necessity of righteousness, is set forth. "We know that whosoever is begotten of God sinneth not." Thus John rebukes the Christian who is careless of conduct, and the cynic who sneers at virtue. However, he also warns the believer that he is fighting a sleepless foe, and that victory can be secured only by ceaseless effort; but it can be secured: "he that was begotten of God keepeth himself, and the evil one toucheth him not."

b. The reality of the "new birth" is next declared: "We know that we are of God, and the whole world lieth in the evil one." The believer does possess a life which God himself has imparted: it may be undeveloped, but it consists in a principle and germ which forever separate and distinguish him from the whole unbelieving world that lies in the power of the evil one.

c. "We know that the Son of God is come." We believe in the divine mission of Jesus Christ. If life has been imparted, if righteousness is possible, it is because we have come to know God, and to enjoy fellowship with God as he has been revealed to us "in his Son Jesus Christ."

Finally John makes a comprehensive affirmation and adds an affectionate word of warning: "This is the true

God," this God whom Christ has revealed, and he is "eternal life," its Source, its Sustainer, and its Perfecter. It is his gift.

Therefore, "little children, guard yourselves from idols," from all the vain conceptions of God held among men, from all human substitutes for God, from all that might turn you from God; for he is perfectly manifested in Jesus Christ, his Son.

THE SECOND EPISTLE OF JOHN

THE SECOND EPISTLE
OF JOHN

Hospitality is variously regarded as a "fine art," a joyous privilege, an unwelcome necessity, or an opportunity for display. New Testament writers emphasize its importance as a Christian grace, and as a species of evangelistic service. It forms the subject of two inspired letters, the Second Epistle and the Third Epistle of John. These are, it is true, very short letters, and they do contain other messages; but the supreme purpose of II John is to caution Christians against extending hospitality to certain enemies of the church, while III John was written to commend a Christian for his generous hospitality to representatives of the apostle who were traveling evangelists.

It is easy to understand why, in the days of the early church, this was a matter of such deep concern. The proper use of hospitality conditioned the spread of the gospel. This was an age of travel. Christians were moving about continually, over the superb Roman roads, either on private business or as missionary workers. Places of entertainment, however, were difficult to find. The hotel is a comparatively modern institution. Ancient inns were not usually of good repute. Frequently these travelers were poor; in any event, they hesitated to place themselves under obligations to unbelievers. It was necessary, therefore, that Christians should open their homes and welcome as guests many strangers, especially such as came to them bearing the adored "Name." It is evident that such hospitality was a direct and potent means of furthering the gospel and of extending the influence of the church. It is also evident that this hospitality was open to abuse, not only by improvident and unworthy travelers, but particularly by false teachers who, under the guise of a Christian profession, concealed their real opposition to the Christian faith, and endeavored to corrupt and pervert the doctrines taught by the apostles. As a warning against such heretical teachers and against such an abuse of hospitality this letter was written.

It was penned, however, in no spirit of narrowness or harshness or bigotry. Its characteristic word is "love"; it breathes the broadest charity; and it reiterates that "old commandment" which Christ has made new: "that we love one another." Still, there is a second word which is hardly less prominent and no less vital: it is the word "truth." Love must not be allowed to lapse into sentimental softness and weak indifference, particularly when truth is at stake. False teachers are not to be countenanced and courted and publicly entertained.

The particular form of error propagated by those to whom the writer refers, relates to the person of Christ. It denies that he was truly God and truly man, in the mystery of his unique being. One who held such perverted and "advanced" doctrine is declared by John to be "the deceiver and the antichrist." Such a public and professional teacher of error was not to be received into a Christian home. He was to be given no greeting, lest, by courtesy and hospitality, support might be afforded to his evil cause. Such is the burden of this brief epistle; and it closes with the expressed hope that at no distant date the writer may himself be welcomed by those Christian friends to whom the letter is being sent.

The outline of the epistle is as follows:

1. The Salutation *II John 1-3*
2. The Counsel and Warning *Vs. 4-11*
3. The Conclusion *Vs. 12-13*
    a. The Promised Visit. *V. 12*
    b. The Closing Greeting *V. 13*

I
THE SALUTATION
II John 1-3

1 The elder unto the elect lady and her children, whom I love in truth; and not I only, but also all they that know the truth; 2 for the truth's sake which abideth in us, and it shall be with us for ever: 3 Grace, mercy, peace shall be with us, from God the Father, and from Jesus Christ, the Son of the Father, in truth and love.

It seems certain that this charming little letter comes to us from the hand of John, "the disciple whom Jesus loved." In his First Epistle he has embodied substantially eight of these thirteen verses, while the style and the subject matter are evidently his own. He calls himself simply "the elder," which indicates marked humility in one who was the most eminent member of the Christian church, one who might have styled himself, at least, "the apostle." This modest title, however, may carry with it the suggestion of age, for the writer has outlived all his fellow apostles, and his words are weighty with the experiences of years; and, further, the word "elder" designated a high office in the Christian communion and was claimed by Peter as a mark of distinction. It may thus be concluded that John writes with the authority of age, of official position, and of a personal knowledge of Christ.

"The elect lady," to whom the letter is addressed may have been, as most modern scholars suppose, not an individual but a church, not a person but a Christian society. This conjecture, however, cannot be definitely established. Moreover, the obvious meaning of Scripture is usually the correct meaning and there is nothing in the simple content of the letter actually to discredit the popular view that the phrase denotes some Christian woman of distinguishing gifts and graces. "Her children" are united with her in the salutation, so that, in either case, it is evident that in this epistle more persons than one are addressed. Nor is the question of supreme importance, for it becomes evident that a message is herein contained which is applicable to all Christians and to all churches.

For this household or Christian society John expresses his true affection, which he declares is felt also by all who hold the truth, as it springs from a common faith. It is indeed this united acceptance of Christian verities which ever forms the firm basis of abiding friendships. Such friendships will endure; for this fellowship with the truth is imperishable: "it shall be with us for ever."

The three terms which form the substance of the greeting, "grace, mercy, peace," appear in the opening formula of other epistles, and because of their familiarity are in danger of losing their deep significance. They include all the blessings known to believers, from their source in the "unmerited favor" of God, to their ultimate issue in the peace "which passeth all understanding." Here the enjoyment of these blessings is not, as usual, the substance of a prayer, but of a prediction: "shall be with us"; it is ascribed to the Father but also to Jesus Christ, who is here designated as "the Son of the Father"; it is conditioned upon a right state of mind and heart, "in truth and love"; for the experience is only for those who accept Christ as the divine Son of God, and walk in love toward him and toward their fellowmen. Thus "truth and love," which do not commonly occur in opening salutations, are the distinguishing words in this greeting; and significantly so, for they are the essential words of the epistle which follows.

II
THE COUNSEL
AND WARNING
Vs. 4-11

4 I rejoice greatly that I have found certain of thy children walking in truth, even as we received commandment from the Father. 5 And now I beseech thee, lady, not as though I wrote to thee a new commandment, but that which we had from the beginning, that we love one another. 6 And this is love, that we should walk after his commandments. This is the commandment, even as ye heard from the beginning, that ye should walk in it. 7 For many deceivers are gone forth into the world, even they that confess not that Jesus Christ cometh in the flesh. This is the deceiver and the antichrist. 8 Look to yourselves, that ye lose not the things which we have wrought, but that ye receive a full reward. 9 Whosoever goeth onward and abideth not in the teaching of Christ, hath not God: he that abideth in the teaching, the same hath both the Father and the Son. 10 If any one cometh unto you, and bringeth not this teaching, receive him not into your house, and give him no greeting: 11 for he that giveth him greeting partaketh in his evil works.

The letter opens, like many of Paul's epistles, with an expression of joy in the consistent life of Christian believers. The writer has found certain men in the church, certain "children" of "the elect lady" to whom the letter is written, "walking in truth," that is to say, "actually," or "really," as God has commanded. Surely no pastor has a more exalted cause for rejoicing than to find such true life manifested by the members of his flock.

To encourage such living on the part of his readers, John exhorts them to Christian love, which, in one sense, is not "a new commandment," for it was strikingly set forth in the law of Moses; yet, in another sense it is "new," for Christ has given a new standard and a new example and a new motive to love. John further reminds us that the real exercise of love will result in keeping all the commandments of God: "And this is love, that we should walk after his commandments." Love is ever the fulfilling of the law. Obedience finds its motive in love; obedience is the fruit of love. "That ye should walk in it" has ever been the commandment for all Christians. Right living is certain to result from love.

John has been led thus to encourage the exercise of love, because love so realized in life will be a safeguard against error. It will not prevent one from opposing error. Christian love should not make one indifferent to Christian truth, for if this truth is lost, love will lack its motive and its norm. Thus John comes to the very heart of his message in the warning against the false teachers, many in number, who are endangering the faith and so the life of believers.

They were once nominal members of the church but have "gone forth into the world"; in every age the most dangerous of all delusions and denials of truth have come from those who have been acquainted with Christianity, who have claimed to hold many of its doctrines, who have cloaked themselves under its name, who have used its phrases, who even have followed its forms.

These false teachers are called "deceivers," for they lead to false living as well as to false views of truth. Belief and life are inseparable. Faith always manifests itself in works. Corrupt doctrine inevitably results in corrupt morals. The vital error of these "deceivers" related to the person of Christ. They denied that he is at once truly man and truly God. They were the first in the long line of heretics who, under various names, have refused to accept this cardinal truth of Christianity. There is something very striking in the phrase used by John: "They confess not that Jesus Christ cometh in the flesh." The divine humanity ever continues and will again be manifest; but were Christ only a man, then his claims were untrue, his death also would have no saving power. Nothing could be more fatal than to deny either his true humanity or his essential deity.

Such teachers John condemns in unsparing terms. One who advocates their errors is declared to be not only a deceiver of men, but also an enemy of Christ. He is animated by the spirit of that last great deceiver of mankind, that "man of sin," that "antichrist," who will yet appear to oppose himself to God, and to be destroyed by the personal appearing of the returning, divine, victorious Christ. Because of the presence and the perilous influence of such false teachers, Christians need to be on their guard lest they lose the faith and the hope and the love which have come to them through the labors of true teachers; they need to watch and to persevere that, when Christ appears, they may receive for their steadfastness a full and complete reward.

Such watchfulness is the more necessary because these teachers make proud claims of being "advanced" and "progressive" and "leaders of new thought"; whereas, in fact, those who deny the teachings of Christ about his person and his saving work have fallen back into darkness, and have lost nothing less than God himself, for one cannot know God or live in a vital relation to him or enjoy conscious fellowship with him, in case he rejects the revelation which God has made of himself in Christ. It is far better to seem "behind the times" than to be without the truth. True progress consists in retaining the realities which the past has assured, and in growing in the knowledge of Christ. His teachings cannot be contradicted or abandoned as out of date. They may be explored and explained and applied, but they set limits of revealed truth which no one may disregard: "He that abideth in the teaching, the same hath both the Father and the Son."

These false teachers are the more dangerous because they often move in the best circles of society, and are of pleasing personality, and claim the name of "Christian." Their presence at public gatherings, their participation in social and civic movements, raise questions of extreme difficulty and delicacy. The advice of John is uncompromising; "If any one cometh unto you, and bringeth not this teaching, receive him not into your house, and give him no greeting: for he that giveth him greeting partaketh in his evil works." We should note at once, however, that the reference here is to teachers who claimed to be official and authoritative, and to such treatment of them as plainly would indicate sympathy with their errors and support of their professed efforts to overthrow fundamental truth. John does not forbid ordinary courtesy, he does not encourage impoliteness or churlishness or unkindness or cruelty. It must be remembered that the provision of hospitality was, in the days of the early church, a definite means of furthering the gospel; but it might quite as easily be used to help in the spread of error. It is against such a wrong use of hospitality that John here protests. He means that professional, recognized teachers of heresy are not to be aided in their efforts, are not to be recognized as entitled to support, are not to be so welcomed and greeted as to be encouraged in their work. Truth is not to be sacrificed even in the name of love.

III
THE CONCLUSION
Vs. 12-13

12 Having many things to write unto you, I would not
write them *with paper and ink: but I hope to come unto*
you, and to speak face to face, that your joy may be made
full. 13 The children of thine elect sister salute thee.

John has given his counsel of Christian love, he has
sounded his warning against compromising essential truth;
he now adds that there are many other matters, of real
importance to his readers, which he would gladly communicate; however, he finds writing with paper and ink
to be unsatisfactory, and he is consoled with the expectation of an approaching visit when he can speak with his
friends "face to face"; he is certain that they will share in
his joy at such a meeting.

Possibly it is reassuring to Christians of the present day
to remember that they have apostolic sympathy in their
dissatisfaction with pen and ink as means of communicat-
ing with those they love. Surely there is much that is
more satisfying in speaking "face to face," or as we should
say, "heart to heart." However, even a letter is prefer-
able to complete isolation, and surely the world would be
much poorer had the aged apostle refrained from sending
to his friends this epistle which tells us that we are to walk
in love and to abide in the truth, if we are to enjoy grace
and mercy and peace "from God the Father, and from
Jesus Christ, the Son of the Father." The final salutation
is from the members of a household or church related to
those to whom the epistle has been penned, and it adds
another touch to the assurance of fellowship which all enjoy who are united in their acceptance of Christian truth.

THE THIRD EPISTLE OF JOHN

THE THIRD EPISTLE
OF JOHN

This precious little fragment of the past may well engage our thoughtful review, for it contains pen portraits from the apostolic age which the passing of centuries has not dimmed, which reflect the life of the early church, and which bring to Christians of every age and land messages of encouragement and warning and cheer.

The first of the portraits is that of Gaius, apparently a wealthy householder, whose Christian faith has been shown by his generosity toward his Christian friends and particularly by the hospitality he has shown to certain traveling evangelists or preachers. These brethren were strangers to him; but "for the sake of the Name" he has received them into his own home, and this, too, in spite of evident opposition from a prominent member of the church who attempted to prevent this exercise of Christian courtesy. To him the aged apostle John writes this letter, to commend him for his gracious hospitality and to encourage him to speed these visiting messengers on their journey, and that, too, in a manner "worthily of God," and worthily of their sacrifice and worthily of their high service. The picture of Gaius is thus that of a consistent, spiritual, charitable believer, who by the grace of hospitality is strengthening the church and furthering the gospel of Christ.

The second portrait is that of Diotrephes, a man whose pride of place and pride of intellect threaten to wreck the peace and prosperity of the Christian communion. In his presumptuous self-confidence, he has opposed the teaching and the authority of the aged and revered apostle. He has given no heed to the message of John, he has attacked him maliciously "with wicked words," he has refused hospitality to his messengers, and has attempted to exclude from the church those who were to receive these messengers into their homes. It is a pitiful picture of overweening ambition, of conceit, of arrogance, of tyranny, and of the love and abuse of power.

There is a third sketch. It is of one, Demetrius, who appears to be the bearer of the letter, a man held in universal esteem by his fellow Christians, whose life accords with his profession, who has the special commendation of the inspired apostle John.

Underneath these last two pictures John writes a significant motto: "Beloved, imitate not that which is evil, but that which is good."

Such are the three pen portraits contained in this little letter; but in sketching them the writer has drawn unconsciously a picture of himself. We see him bending under the weight of years, burdened with the care of the churches, sustained by love for Christ and his cause, comforted by the sympathy and devotion of faithful friends, zealous for the spread of the gospel, boldly rebuking error and ready to discipline offenders, but tender in his affections and confident in the triumph of truth.

No less striking is the picture of the early church which the epistle portrays. It appears as a household of brethren, united by bonds of Christian love, separated from the unbelieving world, extending its influence by unselfish service and by gracious hospitality, not free, however, from the perils of ambition and jealousy and faction among its members, but guarded and guided by men of apostolic gifts and graces, strong in love, rejoicing in truth, devoted to Christ.

The letter might be outlined as follows:

1. The Salutation and the Writer's Joy   *III John 1-4*
2. The Praise of Gaius   *Vs. 5-8*

I
THE SALUTATION
AND THE WRITER'S JOY

III John 1-4

1 The elder unto Gaius the beloved, whom I love in truth.

2 Beloved, I pray that in all things thou mayest prosper and be in health, even as thy soul prospereth. 3 For I rejoiced greatly, when brethren came and bare witness unto thy truth, even as thou walkest in truth. 4 Greater joy have I none than this, to hear of my children walking in the truth.

The aged apostle John, long a prisoner on Patmos, now laboring in Ephesus and burdened with the care of the churches of Asia, had much to cause him anxiety, sorrow, and disappointment; he was sustained, however, by his invincible faith in Christ, he was comforted by close human friendships, and most of all was he cheered by learning of the loyal and consistent lives of those who, as a result of his ministry, had been turned from paganism to become fruitful and helpful servants of the Lord. Among the latter was Gaius, to whom this letter was addressed. The name is familiar, and appears in three other New Testament passages; but it is unnecessary, if not impossible, to identify this Gaius with any one of the Christian disciples who bore the same name. Probably all that can be learned of him is contained in the few verses which follow. He seems to have been a man of considerable wealth, prominent in the church to which he belonged, faithful to his Christian profession, and specially to be commended for the hospitality he had shown to traveling evangelists who represented John and the church.

The "salutation" addressed to him is unusually brief; but John, who styles himself "the elder," calls Gaius "the beloved," and declares that he loves him "in truth." Even so brief a greeting thus contains the two words which characterize the Second and the Third Epistle of John, namely, "truth" and "love." The accent upon these words differs slightly in the two letters, but by them the letters are molded and united. In the second letter, while love is enjoined, there is warning against a weak tolerance of those who denied the truth; in this Third Epistle, love is praised for its exercise toward those who proclaimed the truth. The Second Epistle condemns the departure from the truth which is known as "heresy"; the Third Epistle condemns the lack of love among professing Christians which results in "schism."

If the salutation is brief, its real content is enlarged by the prayer which immediately follows and which takes the place of the more usual greeting of "grace, mercy, peace." This prayer is quite extraordinary in its content. In the opening of no other New Testament epistle is there recorded a petition for temporal blessings and for physical health: "Beloved, I pray that in all things thou mayest prosper and be in health." It would appear that Gaius had been ill. What is specially remarkable, however, is the measure of prosperity which John proposes: "even as thy soul prospereth." The prayer is that the temporal prosperity of Gaius may be as great as his spiritual welfare and that his body may be as well as his soul. Few of us dare offer that prayer; by most Christians the terms need to be reversed. The proof of his spiritual prosperity is found in the report which has come of the generosity shown by Gaius. This fact is also the warrant for the prayer: Gaius has already made such a wise use of his temporal blessings that the apostle feels justified in asking that his resources may be enlarged, as he also prays that his health may be improved.

Such a report of the faithful stewardship of Gaius has

afforded to John the greatest joy. The news has been brought by fellow Christians who seem to have come, not once only, but from time to time, with the same tidings. The substance of their message is declared by John to be a "witness unto thy truth," by which he means that they are testifying to the fact that Gaius is showing his acceptance of Christian truth by his Christian life, he is manifesting his faith by his works, or as John adds, "even as thou walkest in truth," that is, consistently, "truly."

The word "thou" is emphatic; it implies a contrast: there are others whose walk does not correspond to their words; they are not loyal to their profession of faith; from their opposition both Gaius and John have suffered; of these the apostle will speak later; but he now wishes to express to Gaius the extreme gratification which his fidelity to the truth has occasioned: "Greater joy have I none than this, to hear of my children walking in the truth." By his "children" John of course means those believers who have been brought into the Christian life by his influence. Nothing gives him greater gladness than to learn that such are "walking in the truth." In the New Testament John alone uses the last phrase; but the idea is familiar. It denotes living in the sphere of revealed truth, allowing it to dominate and to control the mind and the soul, to mold the character and to determine all choices and all acts. Surely no greater joy could be experienced by a Christian worker than to learn that those whom he has brought to Christ are thus "walking in the truth."

II
THE PRAISE OF GAIUS
Vs. 5-8

5 Beloved, thou doest a faithful work in whatsoever thou doest toward them that are brethren and strangers withal; 6 who bare witness to thy love before the church: whom thou wilt do well to set forward on their journey worthily of God: 7 because that for the sake of the Name they went forth, taking nothing of the Gentiles. 8 We therefore ought to welcome such, that we may be fellow-workers for the truth.

The act which occasioned this letter, and which John specially desires to praise, is that of extending hospitality to certain missionaries who had been sent from Ephesus to minister to the church of which Gaius was a member. It is easily understood how necessary it was for Christians, in that age particularly, to exercise the grace of hospitality, and how greatly this grace tended to further the gospel. For two reasons, however, Gaius was to be specially commended: first, because the itinerant preachers whom he had welcomed to his home were total strangers to him; and, secondly, because his kindness made him the object of criticism and opposition and ill will on the part of members of his own church. His act is therefore called "a faithful work," both because it was an expression of his sincere belief, and also because it required steadfastness and courage in its accomplishment. This expression of Christian loyalty was one of those which had been reported to John, and, as he declares, the messengers who had been so befriended "bare witness to thy love before the church." Now these same messengers are returning to Gaius, and John makes bold to request that Gaius not only shall entertain them but shall aid them on their further journey by gifts of money and provisions, and that, too, in the most liberal manner, or, as John says, with a generosity "worthily of God."

Two reasons are assigned for such gracious generosity. One is the fact that these messengers are representatives of Christ and are going forth to make Christ known. It is true that the word, "Christ," is not mentioned; it does not occur once in this letter. "They went forth," John declares, "for the sake of the Name"; but there is no doubt what name is meant: it is "the name which is above every name," in which some day every knee shall bow.

The second reason for this kindness is the practice of these particular missionaries, who, to avoid all appearance of selfishness and all suspicion of unworthy motives in preaching, refused to accept hospitality or remuneration from the Gentiles to whom they were bringing the gospel.

There is also a third reason mentioned by John, as applying not to this particular case alone, or to these special missionaries, but to all Christians in every age: "We therefore ought to welcome such, that we may be fellow-workers for the truth." By extending sympathy and support to the ministers and messengers and missionaries of Christ, we are sharing in their work of making known the truth of Christ; and as we participate in their labor and their toil and their sacrifice, so, too, we shall share in their rejoicing and their reward.

III
THE CONDEMNATION
OF DIOTREPHES
Vs. 9-10

> *9 I wrote somewhat unto the church: but Diotrephes,*
> *who loveth to have the preëminence among them, receiveth*
> *us not. 10 Therefore, if I come, I will bring to remem-*
> *brance his works which he doeth, prating against us with*
> *wicked words: and not content therewith, neither doth he*
> *himself receive the brethren, and them that would he for-*
> *biddeth and casteth them out of the church.*

In striking contrast with Gaius stands Diotrephes; and
as the former receives unstinted praise, the latter is given
an unqualified rebuke. The very name Diotrephes, which
has been translated "nursling of Zeus" (the king of the
gods), may indicate some boasted aristocracy of birth or
social connection, and may be related to the pride and
vanity of this man who so loved "to have the preëmi-
nence." He was insolent toward John, whose apostolic
authority he should have respected, and overbearing
toward his fellow believers, for whose welfare he had no
regard. John had written a brief letter to the local church
of which Diotrephes was a member; but the letter had been
suppressed by him, or at least its authority had been denied and its counsels had been neglected. This was in
effect a rejection of the apostle, or, as John says, "Diotrephes . . . receiveth us not." He had gone even farther, and had made an open attack upon the apostle,
"prating" against him "with wicked words." These words
may have been light and reckless, mere "bubbles" as the
term denotes; but they were inspired by malice and they

were accompanied by deeds no less distressing: "Neither doth he himself receive the brethren, and them that would he forbiddeth and casteth them out of the church." The "brethren" thus cruelly treated were the actual representatives of the apostle, the messengers of Christ and his church, and the influence of Diotrephes was so great as thus to threaten the progress of the gospel. No wonder that John writes to commend Gaius, who in such a crisis has shown his loyalty to the truth by extending hospitality to the brethren; and no wonder that he here states in reference to Diotrephes, "If I come, I will bring to remembrance his works," by which he meant that they would be rebuked and punished. Thus John draws the picture of one of the first in the long line of men whose ambition and greed of power have imperiled the peace and progress of the Christian church; the pen may be in the trembling hand of an aged apostle, but its strokes are true and the sketch is vivid. It is just possible that the apostle may have recalled an earlier experience of his own when with his brother James he had sought for a place of preeminence. Surely some modern readers need to be reminded that envy and pride and selfish ambition are far removed from the spirit of him who "came not to be ministered unto, but to minister, and to give his life a ransom for many."

IV

THE COMMENDATION
OF DEMETRIUS

Vs. 11-12

11 Beloved, imitate not that which is evil, but that which is good. He that doeth good is of God: he that doeth evil hath not seen God. 12 Demetrius hath the witness of all men, and of the truth itself: yea, we also bear witness; and thou knowest that our witness is true.

To counteract the influence of Diotrephes which is imperiling the belief and order of the church, John is sending a messenger, by the name of Demetrius. He is the bearer of this letter, and is strongly commended to Gaius, to whom the letter is written and by whom he is to be entertained. This commendation is threefold: first, "Demetrius hath the witness of all men," that is his work in the church is widely known and is everywhere approved; secondly, he has the witness "of the truth itself," that is, the manifestation in life and word of the effect of accepted truth, shows him to be worthy of trust and affection; thirdly, the aged and inspired apostle, John, adds his word of personal testimony to the character of this loyal and popular minister of the early church: "Yea, we also bear witness; and thou knowest that our witness is true."

This commendation is introduced by a precept of wide-reaching application, and by a statement of deep significance: "Beloved, imitate not that which is evil, but that which is good." Thus Gaius is warned against the example and influence of Diotrephes whose character has just been sketched, and is exhorted to emulate the zeal and fidelity of Demetrius who is now to be introduced. How-

ever, John first adds the characteristic words: "He that
doeth good is of God: he that doeth evil hath not seen
God." That is to say, one whose habit of life is right, one
who practices what is good, shows that he has been "born
of God"; but one whose life is evil has not caught that
transforming vision of God, in the face of Jesus Christ,
which is possible to the eye of faith. No matter what one
may profess or what power he may possess in the church,
words and deeds are the infallible proofs of the real but
hidden springs of life.

V
THE CONCLUSION
Vs. 13-14

13 I had many things to write unto thee, but I am unwilling to write them to thee with ink and pen: 14 but I hope shortly to see thee, and we shall speak face to face. Peace be unto thee. The friends salute thee. Salute the friends by name.

As the aged apostle brings his letter to a close, just before writing his benediction of "peace," and before sending the greetings of Christian friends in Ephesus to the Christian friends of Gaius, he states how irksome and unsatisfactory it is for him to communicate "with ink and pen," and he expresses the hope of a coming visit when he can "speak face to face." It is these natural and human touches which make the last epistles of John so fascinating and full of life. Here we are not moving in the sphere of the supernatural and mysterious; there is no suggestion of miracle and marvel; but here we find men and women like ourselves, tempted by human weakness and faults, furthering the work of Christ by the exercise of hospitality, living in the power of a vital faith, laboring in love and "walking in the truth."

THE EPISTLE OF JUDE

THE EPISTLE OF JUDE

The writer calls himself "Jude" and adds that he is "brother of James." Both names were common among the early followers of Christ. Two of the apostles bore the name of "Jude," or its exact equivalent "Judas," and two others were called "James." Neither this writer, however, nor his brother were members of the apostolic band. This James was probably the well-known leader of the church in Jerusalem and a brother of our Lord. It therefore appears that the last of the General Epistles, like the first, was composed by a member of that family circle which is reverently associated with the memories of Nazareth, of Mary, the mother of Jesus, and of our blessed Lord himself.

The occasion of the epistle seems to have been the reception by the writer of news concerning the peril which was threatening the church. He had been addressing himself to the task of writing a treatise on the subject of the "salvation" which he shared with his fellow Christians, when he unexpectedly found it necessary to write them this message in which he urges them "to contend earnestly for the faith which was once for all delivered unto the saints." He has learned that entrance into the church has been gained by certain godless men who, in the name of liberty, are living in lawless license, and under the cloak of a Christian profession are hiding their shameless impurity. Both by word and by deed they are denying the Lord Jesus Christ.

Jude declares that their doom will be as certain as that of the unbelieving Israelites, or of the fallen angels, or of Sodom and Gomorrah. He describes them as insolently defiant of all authority, like Cain in murderous envy, like Balaam in their greed and seduction, like Korah in their pride and rebellion. They threaten their fellow Christians with shipwreck both of faith and morals. In their false pretensions they are like shepherds which feed themselves and forget the flock, like clouds which bring no rain, like fruitless trees. Restless and noisy as the surf which breaks on the shore, they produce only that which is their shame. Like blazing meteors, they appear brilliant for a time but are plunging into eternal night.

In reference to them, Jude quotes a prophecy attributed to Enoch, which declares the coming of the Lord in judgment upon these men or upon the sinners of his own day. Like the latter, these apostates complain of their lot, live in sensual indulgence, boast of their knowledge and powers, and selfishly seek their own advancement.

The readers are reminded that the apostles of Christ had also predicted that the end of his age would be marked by the appearance of just such false leaders who would follow their own lusts, destroy the unity of the church, and walk after their fleshly desires, not according to the guidance of the Holy Spirit.

In view of such perilous influences, Jude urges upon true believers steadfast effort in Christian growth, continual prayer, confidence in the love of God, and abiding hope in the appearing of Christ who will bring their experience of grace to its final glory. As to those who are in danger of being corrupted by the false teachers, some are to be convinced by argument, some are to be saved from their peril by severe discipline, some are to be regarded with pity while their polluting contact is shunned. The epistle closes with a superb doxology which reminds the readers of the unfailing protection and the saving power of God, to whom, with Christ our Lord, is ascribed eternal praises.

The outline of the epistle is as follows:

1. The Salutation   *Jude 1-2*
2. The Occasion of Writing   *Vs. 3-4*
3. The Sin and the Doom of the False Teachers
   Vs. 5-16
4. The Exhortation to the Faithful   *Vs. 17-23*
5. The Doxology   *Vs. 24-25*

I

THE SALUTATION

Jude: 1-2

*1 Jude, a servant of Jesus Christ, and brother of James,
to them that are called, beloved in God the Father, and
kept for Jesus Christ: 2 Mercy unto you and peace and
love be multiplied.*

The writer of this epistle was, almost certainly, a brother
of our Lord Jesus; yet with unassumed modesty he calls
himself "a servant of Jesus Christ, and brother of James."
As, however, this James was probably the well-known
head of the church at Jerusalem and brother of the Lord,
Jude does intimate his relation to Jesus and further suggests that his words are worthy of deep respect. He indicates, however, that his human kinship to Christ is less
important to him than his spiritual relation, by the first
phrase he employs, "a servant of Jesus Christ." The
word is literally a "bondservant" or "slave." Possibly
there is something of humility in the term, but there is
surely much of dignity. The same title was claimed by
the great apostle Paul. It may be assumed properly by
every follower of Christ. Each one belongs to him, as
purchased by his precious blood, each owes to him submission, each finds his chief joy in his service.

The persons addressed are unnamed and unknown; but
the terms in which they are described are so beautiful that
all readers may rejoice in believing that such phrases belong to them if only they belong to Christ. They are
"called," for they have heard and heeded the gracious
summons to salvation given by the Holy Spirit; they are
"beloved," but the love is more than human sentiment
and is due to their special relation to "God the Father";

they are being "kept," not merely through present trials and temptations, but "for Jesus Christ" whose glorious return they are awaiting. For such favored persons, whose blessings are related to Father, Son, and Holy Spirit, the unique prayer is offered: "Mercy unto you and peace and love be multiplied." "Mercy" is that favor toward the undeserving shown by the Father. "Peace" denotes a perfect relation toward God and our fellowmen. "Love" is the deepest and most blessed experience of the human soul. It is encouraging to believe that such graces are certain to be increased for all who are loyal to the living Christ.

II
THE OCCASION
OF THE WRITING
Vs. 3-4

*3 Beloved, while I was giving all diligence to write unto
you of our common salvation, I was constrained to write
unto you exhorting you to contend earnestly for the faith
which was once for all delivered unto the saints. 4 For
there are certain men crept in privily, even they who were
of old written of beforehand unto this condemnation, ungodly men, turning the grace of our God into lasciviousness, and denying our only Master and Lord, Jesus Christ.*

While Jude was planning to write his fellow believers a
letter on subjects related to the salvation which they all
shared, he was confronted with the necessity of abandon-
ing this plan, and of preparing this epistle in which he
could urge his readers to a faithful defense of the great
truths which had been received from Christ and his apostles, which he had been hoping to expound, which were
now in grave peril. The nature of this peril was the presence and influence, within the church, of certain men who,
by their teaching as well as by their lives, were denying the
Lord whom they professed to obey. Their coming had
been predicted long ago, but their entrance into the
church had been unobserved, or their real nature had not
been known, and their power had not been appreciated.
Now, however, Jude is fully aroused to the menace which
they constitute to the Christian faith, and he sounds a call
to arms, he declares that the enemy is really entrenched
within the camp, he insists that believers must "contend
earnestly for the faith which was once for all delivered
unto the saints."

By these words he indicates that the body of revealed truth is complete and final. There is no other gospel, there will be none. Its content will be more fully understood, its implications will be developed, its predictions will be fulfilled; but it will never be supplemented or succeeded or supplanted.

Jude further indicates that this truth must be defended. Even in the days of the apostles, even in the early church where truth was held so dear, there were those who denied the realities concerning the unique person and the saving work of Christ, whose insidious teachings corrupted the pure gospel, whose impious lives were concealed by a loud profession of "advanced" knowledge. So it has ever been in all ages. The most dangerous attacks upon the truth have come from within the church itself, and there never have been wanting those who have declared the gospel to be erroneous, defective, or at least immature, who under forms most specious and plausible have attacked "the faith which was once for all delivered unto the saints."

Jude also indicates that the best defense of the truth is found in the influence of a holy life. Of course the Christian beliefs must be carefully studied and clearly stated, misrepresentations must be denied, and false charges must be answered, but the way "to contend earnestly for the faith" is not that of physical force or bitter denunciation or social ostracism, but that of consistent living. Truth is certain to manifest itself in life. The false teachers showed their errors by the impurity of their deeds. Those who would defend the faith must show themselves "saints," by which is meant real "believers" or those who are "consecrated to Christ."

III
THE SIN AND THE DOOM
OF THE FALSE TEACHERS
Vs. 5-16

5 Now I desire to put you in remembrance, though ye know all things once for all, that the Lord, having saved a people out of the land of Egypt, afterward destroyed them that believed not. 6 And angels that kept not their own principality, but left their proper habitation, he hath kept in everlasting bonds under darkness unto the judgment of the great day. 7 Even as Sodom and Gomorrah, and the cities about them, having in like manner with these given themselves over to fornication and gone after strange flesh, are set forth as an example, suffering the punishment of eternal fire. 8 Yet in like manner these also in their dreamings defile the flesh, and set at nought dominion, and rail at dignities. 9 But Michael the archangel, when contending with the devil he disputed about the body of Moses, durst not bring against him a railing judgment, but said, The Lord rebuke thee. 10 But these rail at whatsoever things they know not: and what they understand naturally, like the creatures without reason, in these things are they destroyed. 11 Woe unto them! for they went in the way of Cain, and ran riotously in the error of Balaam for hire, and perished in the gainsaying of Korah. 12 These are they who are hidden rocks in your love-feasts when they feast with you, shepherds that without fear feed themselves; clouds without water, carried along by winds; autumn trees without fruit, twice dead, plucked up by the roots; 13 wild waves of the sea, foaming out their own shame; wandering stars, for whom the blackness of darkness hath been reserved for ever. 14 And to these also Enoch, the seventh from Adam, prophesied, saying, Behold, the Lord came with ten thousands of his holy ones, 15 to execute judgment upon all, and to convict all the ungodly of all their works

of ungodliness which they have ungodly wrought, and of all
the hard things which ungodly sinners have spoken against
him. 16 These are murmurers, complainers, walking after
their lusts (and their mouth speaketh great swelling words),
showing respect of persons for the sake of advantage.

The main portion of this epistle is thus concerned with
the character and the punishment of these men whose
presence and influence are such a serious menace to the
truth. A comparison of this section with II Peter (ch. 2)
shows that the two passages are practically identical.
Many modern students have concluded that when Peter
was writing he had this Epistle of Jude before him; other
scholars equally eminent believe that Jude, in composing
his letter, had in hand the work of Peter. Probably it is
unwise to be too positive in asserting the priority of either
epistle. It does seem, however, that the enemies whose
advent Peter predicts are pictured by Jude as already doing
their ruinous work, and that the evils, which were not fullgrown when Peter wrote, have now reached a fatal maturity. It is evident that in spite of their similarity the passages in both epistles contain features which are original
and distinct. Thus the first example of divine punishment cited by Jude is not found in the Second Epistle of
Peter. It is the case of Israel, the chosen people, who in
spite of their peculiar privileges and their miraculous deliverance from Egyptian bondage, lost faith in God, and all
"that believed not" were "destroyed." This example illustrates not only the certainty of doom but the nature of the
men whom Jude is describing. It traces the source of their
sin to unbelief. It teaches us, not merely that high privilege
does not insure one against failure and consequent penalty,
but also the lesson drawn in the Epistle to the Hebrews
from the same historic facts: "Take heed, brethren, lest
haply there shall be in any one of you an evil heart of unbelief, in falling away from the living God."
The second example of divine retribution Jude takes,

not directly from the Old Testament, but from traditions which were current in the writings of his day. The "fall of the angels" is an event shrouded in mystery, but the reference here is evidently intended to illustrate the fatal pride and rebellion which filled the hearts of the apostates whom Jude is denouncing, and again to warn his readers that the most exalted position is no safeguard against sin and doom.

The third example reverts to the history of Genesis, to the infamous immorality and the subsequent destruction of Sodom and the surrounding cities, a reference intended not only to charge with impurity the false teachers to whom Jude refers, but also to warn them of their peril of suffering a like penalty.

These libertines, however, refuse to be warned; and, vainly dreaming that they can safely pursue their unholy course, they treat with insolence the church authorities who would restrain and admonish them. Jude declares that such conduct is condemned by the example of the archangel, Michael, who refrained from railing against even the devil when disputing with him about the body of Moses. Here again the reference is to a tradition about which it is useless to speculate. The practical purpose of Jude is obvious. He rebukes the impious folly of those men who insulted authorities they should have respected, and spoke irreverently of truths which they did not understand, while, in the realm of sensual indulgence, where they were at home, they brought about their own destruction by yielding to animal passions.

To the charge of senseless insolence, Jude adds that of murderous envy and hatred: "they went in the way of Cain"; and further, of corrupting greed, "the error of Balaam; and, again, of proud rebellion," "the gainsaying of Korah."

Such then are seven, at least, of the evil characteristics of these guilty apostates whose destruction Jude solemnly predicts; they are unbelieving, proud, sensual, insolent, envious, greedy, rebellious. Their picture is made more abhorrent, however, by the figures of speech which follow, which portray their corrupting influence, their hypocrisy, their disgrace, and their doom. Partaking of the Christian love feasts, these false teachers are like hidden rocks which cause the shipwreck of souls. In their great professions and their failure to give aid, they are like shepherds who care solely for their own needs, or like clouds which bring no rain, or like trees which are fruitless and blasted, or like waves breaking on the shore and leaving a worthless deposit, or like meteors which for a brief time blaze across the sky and disappear in eternal darkness.

The punishment of these apostates has been intimated again and again; but it is finally stated by Jude in words which tradition had assigned to Enoch, "the seventh from Adam," the ancient saint who "walked with God" and was translated without dying. It is stated that he prophesied "to these," that is, to men of this same character, who lived in his own day, as well as to these false teachers in the early church. It is further implied that exactly such men will exist in the latter days just before our Lord returns, dissatisfied men, slaves of passion, proud boasters, and cringing flatterers. However, the Lord will come "with ten thousands of his holy ones to execute judgment upon all." In the expression, "Behold, the Lord came," we have the past tense of prophetic vision. So certain is the event that the prophet describes it as already fulfilled. The delay may seem long, sinful apostates may feel secure, but the hour will strike, and the Judge surely will appear.

IV

THE EXHORTATION
TO THE FAITHFUL

Vs. 17-23

*17 But ye, beloved, remember ye the words which have
been spoken before by the apostles of our Lord Jesus
Christ; 18 that they said to you, In the last time there shall
be mockers, walking after their own ungodly lusts. 19
These are they who make separations, sensual, having not
the Spirit. 20 But ye, beloved, building up yourselves on
your most holy faith, praying in the Holy Spirit, 21 keep
yourselves in the love of God, looking for the mercy of our
Lord Jesus Christ unto eternal life. 22 And on some have
mercy, who are in doubt; 23 and some save, snatching
them out of the fire; and on some have mercy with fear;
hating even the garment spotted by the flesh.*

Here, at last, the epistle reaches its climax; not in the
description of the false teachers and their doom, but in
this exhortation, addressed to the faithful followers of
Christ, the real purpose of Jude is fulfilled.

The exhortation is threefold. First, Jude reminds his
readers that the presence in the church of such ungodly
men was to be expected; it should not surprise or dismay
or discourage; the apostles of Christ had predicted it.
The church never would be free from such peril before the
Lord returned. One sign of his near approach would be
the increasing power and insolence of such teachers, who
would mock at the idea of a coming judgment, who would
walk according to their godless lusts, who would "make
separations" in the church, men of sensual instincts, utterly
devoid of spiritual life.

In striking contrast with such apostates, Jude next encourages his readers to build themselves up upon the foundation of their "most holy faith," by which he means upon those truths which "once for all" were "delivered unto the saints," which alone form the true basis for an enlarging Christian life and experience. Further, they were to pray in the power and under the guidance of the Holy Spirit from whom alone could come the strength for growth and the power for life. They were to "keep" themselves "in the love of God"; this is the most emphatic verb in this part of the exhortation; it is the one imperative, for to abide in the consciousness of the love of God is the surest safeguard against sin; such abiding may be secured by faith and prayer and obedience. They were to keep their eyes fixed upon the mercy which would be brought to them at the return of Christ, when "eternal life" would be realized by them in all its fullness and glory.

Last of all, Jude exhorts believers as to their attitude toward those who are in danger of being led astray from consistent Christian life and belief. He declares that careful discrimination must be exercised, and that every effort should be made to protect and to save. Some are "in doubt"; they merit your compassion, your warning, your patient care. Some are in imminent peril, they need severe discipline; only thus can they be snatched from the fire of their fierce temptations. Even those whose unbelief and perversity seem most hopeless, are to be regarded with pity by those who shrink from all contact with their pollution and sin.

Thus Jude exhorts Christians how to meet impiety and apostasy; not with surprise, for these have been predicted; not with inactivity, for spiritual zeal and effort form the best protection against temptation; not with indifference, for many souls will be in peril and some may be rescued from death.

V
THE DOXOLOGY
Vs. 24-25

24 Now unto him that is able to guard you from stumbling, and to set you before the presence of his glory without blemish in exceeding joy, 25 to the only God our Saviour, through Jesus Christ our Lord, be glory, majesty, dominion and power, before all time, and now, and for evermore. Amen.

No more inspiring ascription of praise can be found in the General Epistles, nor one with which these epistles more fittingly may conclude. The thought has been led through dark scenes of perplexity and suffering, of apostasy and doom; but now the clouds break away, and the eyes gaze in rapture on the face of a loving God, on the glory of a coming Christ. The readers had been told to "keep" themselves in the love of God; now they are assured that God will keep them; in spite of pitfalls and snares, he "is able to guard you from stumbling"; regardless of moral perils and present sorrows, he will "set you before the presence of his glory," at the appearing of Christ, "without blemish" and in exultant "joy." To this one God our Savior, as there ever has been, so may there be now and forevermore, "glory, majesty, dominion and power," "through Jesus Christ our Lord." "Amen."